OTI
NATIONS

ELIZABETH S. EILER, PH.D.

A Lightworker's
Case Book for
Healing, Spiritually
Empowering, and
Communing
with the
Animal Kingdom

outskirtspress
DENVER, COLORADO

Acknowledgements and Dedications:

I dedicate this book to the Animal Kingdom and all its wise and wonderful members. If the life of even one animal is improved through the reading of this book, then it has served its purpose.

Special thanks to Martha Wittkowski and the exceptional staff and volunteers at Animal Lifeline of Iowa for welcoming me into the amazing world of these special-needs animals and granting permission for their stories to be told.

I am deeply grateful to my many human and animal clients, with special thanks to Stacie Garmon for her permission to tell the story of Cosmo and to Suzette Schmidt for her permission to tell Buddy's story.

To my husband Benjamin and our dog-children Reggie, Jack, and Oscar, I can do no more than to return the unconditional love with which you have always strengthened and encouraged me. I am grateful each day for the circle of blessing that is our family. I also give thanks to my late father, L. Frank Davidson, for his wonderful pencil drawings of animals which appear in this book.

Lastly, I offer honor, love, and thanks to our Divine Source and the Angels, Archangels, and Ascended Masters without whom no healing or reconciliation is possible and to the Spirit Guides and Power Animals who light our path through the Universe.

Contents

The Animals' Plea

Love me as I am.
Have I not taught you to love unconditionally,
to meet anger with affection, to be forgiving,
and to practice hope in the face of adversity?
Love me like I love you, boundlessly, eternally, joyfully.

Ask me.
My trust for you is in my eyes,
for you are wise in your world.
I know the Wild ways and the Deep things.
I am wise in the First World that came before yours.
Let me decide, too. I may surprise you.

Hear me.
I have always been your listening ear,
sharing your hopes and heartaches in my quiet way.
I tell you my wishes and dreams, too. Do you hear them?
I open my secret heart to you in the words of the soul.
Please listen.

Stay with me.
> When I am hurt or sick, I need you,
> for your presence comforts me.
> When I am playful, leaping at the sun, I need you,
> because your nearness makes my happiness complete.
> When I grow tired and feeble and my eyes are dimmed,
> you alone will make me feel safe and loved.
>
> When it is time for me to go, bear me gently to the Angels.
> You have been my guardian – and I will become yours.

For the animal shall not be measured by man. In a world far older and more complete than ours they move finished and complete, gifted with extensions of the senses we have lost or never attained, living by voices we shall never hear. They are not brethren, they are not underlings; they are other nations, caught with ourselves in the net of life and time, fellow prisoners of the splendor and travail of the earth.

— Henry Beston (From *The Outermost House*)

Our Place in the World

For all creatures incarnate on the Earth plane, I believe that there are three basic levels of reality that we all share. (See diagram below).

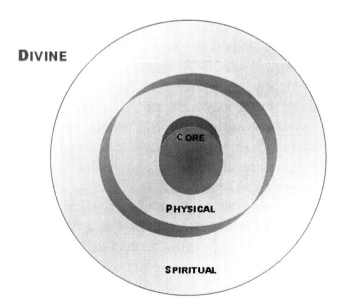

The Universe and everything in it formed from the energetic essence of God, also called Divine Source, Higher Intelligence, The Great Spirit, and many other Names. The Universe began as an emanation of Divine energy, and this energetic building material and all that it comprises possesses the nature of the One from whom it came. As yin and yang are balanced throughout the cosmos, so we see their balance in Divinity with a Father who creates and a Mother who nourishes and enables the creation to live. These are not two gods, but a dualistic God who reflects in Divinity the masculine-feminine dynamic present in all human beings and animals.

At the inner, deeper level of reality, the Earth is a quiet garden. I call this the Core Level. All creatures from the Animal Kingdom, the Plant Kingdom, the Mineral Kingdom, human beings, and all things which live physically are the plants in this garden, the spiritual essence of each contained in an organic form which has its roots in the Earth. In this way, we stand alongside trees and flowers and grass on the face of the Earth, and in groves amongst the forests of coral and anemones under the sea.

This is the form for humans and animals in which the connections of our root chakras are actual roots that penetrate the Earth to draw sustenance from what may be called Mother Earth, Mother Nature, the Divine Feminine, or any other name which appears right to the soul. For me, our Mother in the Earth is part of the feminine face of God. All forms of life at the Core Level exist harmoniously with one another and with our planet, communing in a waking dream of telepathy (which is how plants communicate even in physicality).

Beyond this level is what we know as Physical Reality. We still have roots going down into our Mother in the Earth, but these are perceived metaphysically through the energetic bands of the root chakra. Residing in and being able to move about separately and independently in our physical bodies creates the illusion of separateness from the Earth and her other life forms. Conquering this illusion and developing a clear vision of the Unity of all beings with God is the goal of our fellow seekers on the Path of Enlightenment. Animals have maintained closer physical and emotional ties to the Earth – albeit not in the very literal sense of the members of the Plant Kingdom.

Certain animal species who burrow into the Earth for places of solace or safety, or who inhabit the sheltering arches of caves alongside the spirits of the rocks, are the bridgers between these inner and outer levels of reality. Rabbits, gophers, moles, prairie dogs, wolves, and bears in hibernation all remember and recreate their rootedness in Mother Earth. In the Insect Kingdom, mud daubers and termites build houses out of mud; ants raise their hills; and cicadas spend most of their lives underground, taking flight only to reproduce and then perish. In large part, it is humanity that has forgotten or chosen to deny our connection to Nature.

A more amorphous level of reality beyond the Physical is the Spiritual Realm. As spiritual beings having physical incarnations, this is a realm humans inhabit together with all animals, plants, rocks, waters, and other physical manifestations which house Spirit. We share the Spiritual Realm with the souls of all beings who have left the Earth plane as well as spirit beings who have never inhabited the Earth. We have access to this level of reality at all times. This is where souls emerge and where they return after the death of the physical body.

We simultaneously inhabit all three levels: Core, Physical, and Spiritual. It is our nature to span many worlds. It is also true that we share these realities with creatures of many kinds who have as much claim to them as we do. Just as the realities are united, so we are united with all the beings that inhabit them with us.

Beyond these first three spheres of reality is the Divine Sphere from whence comes the emanation of God. This is the ultimate and highest home of the soul. It is the place where we achieve the highest state of consciousness for an individuated being, the communion with the Christ Consciousness or Divine Collective. This sphere is where we experience true gnosis, a personal, experiential knowledge of God. Communication with this Divine Sphere is also available to us now, in our deepest, transcendent experiences of God.

Where Do They Go?

Do animals have souls? When a beloved animal companion passes away, will we see him again? Do animals return after death? How can we be sure? Do we just think we hear and see their ghosts because we want so much to believe they are with us?

As a Reiki practitioner at a shelter for sick and injured animals, I have been asked these questions by loving, grief-stricken animal caretakers who have had to say goodbye to dogs and cats that had won a special place in their hearts. I have seen the hope in the eyes of bereaved clients for whom I have performed animal mediumship. I have listened to the personal stories of people who believe they have had spiritual visitations from their animals or have experienced an animal rejoining them through reincarnation.

Their hearts need to know and are seeking a primordial truth in a world that has forgotten much of the ancient wisdom. My unequivocal answer to all of these people is: *Yes*, animals have souls, we *will* see them again, and they *do* return. I hope that at least in part this book will address that final desperate need to be sure, to hope, and to believe that the creatures with whom we share such powerful love will endure as will we.

For many people, the love or the loss of an animal often becomes a gateway into a deeper spiritual journey. The most pragmatic of men will begin to question the fundamental nature of being when he is visited by an apparition of his deceased cat or dog companion. The hardest heart softens when exposed to the unconditional love of animals, opening that person to concepts of Divine love and selflessness. Idle theories about mental telepathy solidify into facts when a woman's dogs understand her particular need for comfort after a hard day.

The animals themselves have much to say on these matters. In giving them a voice, I have drawn from my own experiences with animals, both in my personal life and in my animal Reiki practice, as well as the many spiritual encounters with animals that have been related to me by others. In addition, the spiritual traditions of indigenous peoples weave a rich tapestry of animal interaction with humans on many levels.

In my ongoing quest to commune with the Animal Kingdom, I have gone on shamanic journeys and met with Power Animals. I have met animal Spirit Guides in meditation and in dreams and sought deeper knowledge of and more meaningful interaction with these beings. I consulted with both a shamanic healer and a student of shamanism to learn their thoughts about Power Animals and the Animal Kingdom. I studied animal communication with a Shamanic Reiki Master and telepathic animal communicator. Most importantly, I connected with the animals themselves.

I also offer a chronicle of my field experiences in using energy with animals in my professional Reiki practice, my volunteer work at an animal rescue shelter, and with my own animal family. I have learned to work with Tonglen, Reiki, crystals, Spirit Guides, and the Angelic Realms in order to help animals. I have led humans on guided meditation experiences to facilitate communication with their animals, and I have researched and written extensively on the metaphysical nature and needs of animals.

As we shift our human consciousness into a higher gear in the new millennium, it is my goal that we will not forget or ignore the other bright beings with whom we share this planet. We have a duty to bring light and love to animals and assist them in making their own millennial shift – perhaps into a future where they will be accorded by humans the respect and dignity which they so deserve.

Animals and Energy Work

Dynamic healing reveals a great deal about animal spirituality. The metaphysical connection made between humans and animals during energy work is profound and enlightening into the deeper nature of animals. Reiki Master Victoria Swanson teaches that we link with another being's energy field during an energetic treatment, a way of what she calls "plugging in" that yields a wealth of information about that being.

This information can be spiritual in nature, as when making a soul connection with an animal who is nearing or has made his transition, providing palpable clues about the nature of animal souls, life purpose, and afterlife. Animals also share from their soul memories during healing sessions which offer rich insights into animal reincarnation. Performing energy work with animals reinforces at the physical, spiritual, and emotional levels the deep interconnectedness, sovereignty, and sacredness of all life.

I worked with a woman who was convinced that her dog had taken on a major debilitating illness intended for her. After days of the woman experiencing excruciatingly painful headaches, her dog then suffered a stroke. When I communicated with the dog, indeed her first priority was to make sure that the woman was well and cared for. Many people have experienced animal companions being sensitive to the energetic vibrations of illness, and the unconditional loving and protective nature of the animals who share our lives makes them desire to carry our burdens when they can. This makes dynamic healing essential for the wellbeing of our animal companions.

Most animal lovers discover that their companion animals, as well as animals in the wild, are generally flawless judges of character. I have a number of friends whose opinions of people may be shaken or strengthened based on the reactions of their animals. Sometimes, a nod of approval from a particularly selective cat in the family goes further than any human recommendation. Animals read our energy fields well, picking up on love, hate, anger, jealousy, anxiety, friendship, compassion, and a whole range of emotions.

The sensitivity of animals to energy, including negative vibrations from people and other animals in their environment, makes energy work that much more important for these noble creatures. If you feel stressed out and toxic, chances are that the animals who live with you do, too.

All members of the family need energetic clearing and healing from time to time. Part of this healing empowerment for an animal involves giving him the ability to communicate with his people; the frustration of unexpressed feelings and needs can cause dis-ease of the physical and energetic bodies, and a Reiki practitioner or animal telepath can greatly assist in easing this burden.

Healing at all levels is very much a family affair. When the humans are dealing with illness, stress, or family discord, the animals will be impacted as well. They cannot escape this. Animals share our energy fields and our intimate lives, and any fighting, sickness, or sadness in the home is shared by them. Animals will not get well in a vacuum. They serve as an important reminder for the people close to them to seek healing and wholeness for themselves as well.

Reiki

R eiki, or the channeling of Universal Life Force Energy, has been the foundation of my own work with animals, and the energetic connection it provides has opened many portals of insight into animals' lives and the different ways they may choose to use Reiki. Known as a relaxation and healing technique for humans, Reiki energy is recognized and accepted by all living things. Reiki Masters Kathleen Prasad and Elizabeth Fulton state that, "Reiki is a vibrational 'frequency' that is readily understood and appreciated by an animal..." (p. xiv, Fulton and Prasad, 2006)

Received from Divine Source, Reiki is a healing gift to all members of creation. Since it emanates from Source, Reiki energy has an innate intelligence and is able to heal where it is most needed, regardless of whether the recipient has expressed this need to the healer. The practitioner's role is to be a clear channel, an energetic bridge to the Divine Source. In many ways, this makes Reiki a dynamic form of prayer. Entering another's energy field in order to transmit healing Reiki is also a beautiful expression of the true Unity of all life.

Reiki is the name given to a healing touch method developed and codified by Japanese mystic and religious scholar Dr. Mikao Usui based on Divine revelation or experience of Enlightenment. However, this laying on of hands to heal with energy has been practiced for millennia. Indeed, Dr. Usui rediscovered Reiki while seeking the method used by Christ and the Apostles to perform healings.

Via Reiki attunements by a Master, a practitioner receives the Reiki healing symbols which allow the healer to tune in to healing frequencies and vibrations and then channel healing energy to the recipient though the hands. The International Center for Reiki Training offers the following explanation of Reiki: "The word Reiki is made of two Japanese words – Rei which means 'God's Wisdom or the Higher Power' and Ki which is 'life force energy.' So Reiki is actually 'spiritually guided life force energy." ("What is Reiki," n.d.)

Reiki touches all levels of being – physical, emotional, and spiritual – and heals across any distance of space and in all directions of time. Reiki is a healing energetic frequency that is not confined by any boundaries of the physical world. Like radio waves that travel from Earth into the far reaches of the Universe, many people believe that a being's energy field or aura also radiates outward without end, facilitating connection between any geographical points and any period of time. This may be how we connect with Spirit Guides and transitioned souls – through the ever-radiant field of the spirit body or soul body.

Reiki healing sessions cause the body to release endorphins which act as a natural analgesic, allowing energy wasted on suffering to be redirected into healing. There is much scientific evidence to support this and explain the process of endorphins blocking the transmission of pain signals to the central nervous system while simultaneously producing pain-relieving chemicals. This makes Reiki a wonderful drug-free alternative for any animal experiencing acute or chronic pain. Anyone interested in the science of Reiki for pain relief would do well to visit the web site of the World Reiki Association at http://www.worldreikiasso-ciation.org) where many scholarly materials have been compiled.

My first experience with animal Reiki was a series of hands-on treatments with Jack, a German Shorthaired Pointer whom my husband and I rescued from a shelter. We were told that he had lived a life of neglect and isolation, largely ignored in a garage and segregated from the family. He was shy and withdrawn in our home, trying to learn the rules of indoor family life from our other dog, Reggie, and desperately afraid of making a mistake. My intention was to use Reiki for emotional healing to help Jack resolve past unhappiness and grow confident in our love for him.

I was careful to explain Reiki, just speaking to Jack naturally and trusting that he would understand, allowing the energy to flow and letting him know he could take it if he wanted. Unused to being handled, Jack was wary of being hugged or petted, and he often shied away from human hands. I was very surprised when he climbed up beside me on the couch and curled up, par-tially in my lap, getting as close to me and my hands as possible. Clearly, he understood the energy and very much wanted it.

During our session, Jack provided me with detailed informa-tion about his previous person and his living arrangements with him. Clear images were shown of a bleak garage and machine shed where he had been confined, a yard of yellowed overgrown grass and weeds littered with rusted tools and automotive parts, and a youngish man who was the only member of the household to pay attention to Jack – albeit in a passing and cursory fash-ion. I felt Jack's loneliness, his longing to be part of a pack, and his deep sadness at being ultimately rejected and abandoned. I sent Reiki to these issues to heal Jack's broken heart, and I was deeply moved and honored that he had trusted me enough to share his experiences.

I was amazed by the clarity of the images coming to me from Jack. Reiki had created a heart connection between us, a crystalline current along which Jack could express and then release his past traumas and pain. Treating this information with reverence and acting on the intuitive messages I received strengthened a bond of trust between us, and once the pathways of communication had been opened, the process of mutual sharing became easier.

The insights continued as Jack regularly began to seek me out for Reiki, looking at me and climbing up beside me. He was always deeply peaceful during our sessions and took Reiki for as long as it was offered. He even became jealous of Reggie when I offered him Reiki in Jack's presence, actually screaming in protest as if to say, "That's mine!" Jack would not even allow me to do a group session for him and Reggie simultaneously; Jack wanted it all!

His self-confidence noticeably improved after one treatment, and further treatments accelerated his journey out of a shell of fear and into his own personality. This was illustrated dramatically when, during a session, Jack explained why, although he loved playing in the backyard, he would be peeking in at the back door and crying after only a few minutes. He showed me an incident from his past when The Man (his former person) had been outside and Jack had tried to follow The Man into the house. The Man had lifted a black-booted foot and shoved Jack in the chest, knocking him backwards off of the threshold, hollering at him.

Jack shared that it was the rejection that hurt the most, even more than the boot in the chest. Not being wanted had been his greatest source of pain, and it was hard for him to believe that, at Mommy and Daddy's house, he would *always* be welcomed back inside from the yard. Once we knew this, my husband and I were able to comfort and reassure him so that the backyard could be a place of fun, not a source of worry.

Despite all this work, however, another Reiki Master told me of her intuition that Jack still carried a burden of negativity that needed to be released. Over time, he shared with me an experience when he had been in the bed of a pick-up truck while a man had forced himself on or in some way violated a woman seated in the cab. Jack had not known what to do or how to react and had sat helplessly in the truck bed while a horrific interaction occurred between the humans up front. This event significantly traumatized Jack and left him feeling guilty and afraid. It also illustrates how critical the need is for spiritual care of animals who live in close contact to human beings.

Through the loving and healing bond of Reiki, I was able to explain to Jack that he was not to blame for what had happened. Indeed, he had been a second and hidden victim of the man's aggression. Being able to communicate this dark and frightening experience and receive reassurance and love helped loosen this trauma's hold on Jack. Reiki truly helped lift a shadow from his life.

Reiki had provided a great gift to our whole family, allowing us to see into Jack's heart and soul so that we could address the issues that troubled him. The healing energy strengthened his confidence and bolstered his self-esteem while drawing us closer together. The depth of the communication afforded by the Reiki connection was more than I had expected, despite the many depictions of animal Reiki sessions I had read. Reiki drew me into the emotional and spiritual life of animals in a powerful way that profoundly altered the course of my life and my healing work.

As my husband and I launched our metaphysical business, I knew that I wanted to specialize in Animal Reiki. I began volunteering twice a month at Animal Lifeline of Iowa, a no-kill shelter for animals with special needs, spending two to four hours at a time giving Reiki treatments to dogs and cats with serious medical conditions, disabilities, and injuries as well as pregnant and nursing mothers and orphans. This work has proven transformative both for me as well as the animals with whom I've been privileged to work.

The power of Reiki to reach beyond the physical body and address the energetic causes of stress and dis-ease bears testament to the rich emotional and spiritual life of animals. Maxwell, a cat with severe allergies, expressed through Reiki that he feels like a misfit and is "uncomfortable in his own skin" which makes his veterinary treatments less effective. A shelter cat named Amie explained during a Reiki session that numerous failed adoptions were because she wanted to be a companion cat for a man. A sweet Bichon named Teddy failed to respond to heartworm treatment because his "broken heart" from a life of neglect needed to be healed first. Reiki helped all of these animals, reaching deep-seated issues that couldn't be easily communicated to humans.

I've used Reiki to help puppies with separation anxiety, integrate animals into new family situations, empower grieving animals to cope with loss, and speed healing from surgery, injury, and illness. A common issue in the shelter with which Reiki can help is the bewilderment, fear, sadness, and self-blame experienced when an animal is suddenly expelled from her home and separated from family members. I have also used Reiki as a powerful tool for animal communication and animal mediumship. Indeed, Reiki across species ultimately reveals that all of us who share this Earth are far more alike than we are different.

Reiki also shows us palpably that we, humans and animals, have the same God whose love is for all of us. Before the start of one session when I had been asked to perform Reiki to help a family of dogs who were quarreling, I asked for guidance. Jesus instructed me to channel the vibration of love and said that He would do the rest. As I channeled Reiki and tuned into the frequency of love and emotional healing, I knew that He was working for the higher good of the animals and their family. His device was Reiki; I was merely the channel. What a perfect Reiki lesson. What a perfect Reiki prayer.

What is Reiki like for an animal?

To forge a thera- peutic alliance with an animal, start- ing out gently and with mutual re- spect is essential. I introduce myself to an animal and al- low him to become comfortable with  my presence. I explain Reiki and allow energy to flow from my hands so that he can better understand. I tell the animal that I have come to work with him and help with his nerves, fear, digestive problems, or whatever the animal's human has request- ed, and I ask if he would like to receive some Reiki energy.

The animal chooses whether or not to accept Reiki. It is nev- er forced, and indeed, cannot be forced. If the animal does not wish to take the energy, he will simply reject it and allow it to return to Source. As sovereign beings, animals desire to under- stand and choose. In a world where humans make most of their decisions for them, it is very important for me to let the animals know they have freedom of choice with Reiki.

I may place my hands either on or above the body and nev- er touch areas of open wounds or fresh surgery. Sites of injury are only gently touched when appropriate and desired by the animal. Nervous or anxious animals are offered Reiki from a non-threatening distance, and they may choose to come closer to me as treatment progresses.

Reiki always goes to the source of the problem for the ani- mal's highest good and can never cause harm. The animal may feel warmth or coolness, tingling, or deep relaxation. The pro- cess is not painful and is enjoyable. Most animals I have worked with become extremely relaxed during their sessions and usually fall asleep as their bodies gently and naturally assimilate the Reiki energy. Reiki heightens intuition, strengthens the human-animal bond, and makes it easier for animals and humans to communicate.

Animals are able to shift more quickly than humans, and often their sessions are shorter in duration. The animal will let me know when he has had enough Reiki and will move away and disengage from the treatment. Sometimes, animals try a Reiki "sample" and then walk over to a trusted human for encouragement and approval before returning to me for the rest of the session. At other times, the energy flow diminishes, and I know that the animal has received all that is appropriate at that time.

Animals are usually very deeply tranquil during and after Reiki sessions. They may desire a long nap and may also want to drink more water following a session. Reiki induces peace and a heightened sense of wellbeing for animals. Very rarely, animals have a "treatment reaction" which may involve brief cold or 'flu-like symptoms as their bodies eliminate toxins that Reiki has made it easier to shed. They are grateful for this energy work and always find their own unique ways to thank me.

Reiki Case Study: Buster

Buster was a wonderful teacher, highlighting how crucial it is to understand what the animal needs and wants. Buster demonstrated the necessity to ask the animal, "What do you want Reiki to help you with?" rather than barge in with an agenda of healing and fixing what a human thinks is important. The animal knows better than anyone else what he needs, and Buster will always remind me to simply ask the animal what that is. Every time I help an animal transition to a higher plane, Buster's lessons will be with me to help and guide the next little soul.

One of my first shelter clients, Buster was a twelve-year-old Beagle separated by circumstance from his loving person who could no longer care for herself or for him. Dealing with Cushing's syndrome, separation anxiety, and weariness, he was the most depressed dog I had ever seen. Overweight and limping, his little body distorted by an enlarged liver, concerned shelter staff brought him to me for his first treatment.

Animals are great respecters of their own sovereignty as beings. I carefully explained myself to Buster and let him know that he could choose to accept Reiki or not. After a lukewarm reception, he tried a little Reiki and then moved away, meeting every attempt at continued treatment with resistance. I felt like a failure, trying unsuccessfully to press the Reiki while Buster gently but firmly taught me that treatment had to be on his terms or not at all. It was a humbling lesson.

Equally humbling was the one intuitive message I received through the Reiki connection: "Why did she leave me here?" *I explained his person's physical problems and changed circumstances. I asked if he could forgive her for not being as able as they both would have liked. Buster got up and walked away. He was simply not ready.*

Consulting with other Reiki practitioners, we received the insight that Buster was carrying a lot of burdens for his person which had manifested in his unbalanced body. He was tired and wanted to rest, and he was so eager to please, he feared that if he didn't have the energy or the desire to get well and find a new home, he would be letting everyone down. My Reiki Master Teacher asked, "Does he want to die?"

I asked the shelter staff to speak to Buster and tell him that his person was okay and called regularly to see how he was. We let him know she had moved to a new place, and he didn't need to worry or feel responsible anymore. We told him that resting was okay and there was no pressure. He was welcome at the shelter as long as he wanted to stay. At a workshop, an animal telepath advised me that he understood what we had told him and insisted, "I'm okay." He wanted everyone to stop worrying about him!

When I returned to try another session with Buster, I was met with a tearful report. His Cushing's medicine made him violently ill, he had a urinary tract infection unresponsive to antibiotics, and surgery for a likely tumor was not an option. Buster accepted Reiki from me this time because it was offered only to give comfort and love with no expectations or demands.

The veterinarian suspected that Buster had lymphoma. He was suffering, and the hard decision was made to euthanize. Buster needed Reiki to help him transition, and I sought comfort and pain relief, peace, love, healing on whatever levels were appropriate, and strength. We had a close heart connection as he responded to Reiki. Many aspects of his being were engaged, and I saw images of both the puppy and the wolf in his face.

He wanted help to send love to his person and his beloved caregiver at the shelter, and using my heart energies to strengthen his, Buster placed beautiful iridescent flowers of pink and green light, blossoms of love, into their hearts, and as a special thank you, into mine. He wanted to know whether he could be with both his shelter caregiver and his ailing person, and I explained that when he is fully in the Spiritual Realm he can easily be with both of them at once. He didn't want to cause unhappiness. He wanted to be sure his caregiver would be okay.

He worried that he would be lost, not knowing where to go, and I reassured him that he had been there before and knew the way. I asked for Angels and Guardian Spirits to be with him and guide him in his transition. When I placed him into Divine keeping, he was taken into the arms of Mother Mary. Since all his close human relationships had been with women, this seemed very appropriate.

In several sessions leading up to his final moments, Buster let me know that he had already begun the transition process himself. In one session, we connected only at the soul level with no sense of body. In another, he was looking down on his caregiver from above, and in another, his spirit was hovering half in and half out of his body. It comforted the people who loved him to know that they were helping him complete what he had started in his own innate wisdom, and that he was at peace with the circle of life.

I sensed that Buster would be interested in working with me to help other animals at the time of their transitions. It became a matter of waiting for Buster to prepare for this work. A month after Buster's death, a friend's five-year-old Shi Tzu, Baby Sasquatch, died suddenly. I sent Reiki to Baby Sasquatch to help her soul cross over, and I asked if Buster would like to come in with me and assist. Buster responded immediately, coming in strongly and shepherding Baby Sasquatch, making it apparent she was "in good paws."

Buster found a new mission of helping dogs to transition and undertook his role with zeal. The Animal Kingdom was gifted with a wonderful and caring canine spirit helper. It is a privilege to collaborate with him. Sometimes I have called on him, and at other times I have found him already waiting by the side of an ailing dog. He remains a faithful friend.

Animal Chakras and Auras

My work with animals has led me to believe that they have the same seven major energetic centers as human beings, each corresponding to a layer of the auric field, and each vitalizing particular body systems. Some diagrams are drawn with multiple heart chakras for dogs and cats, and different healers have learned to read animals' energy centers in some unique ways. I believe that there is only one heart center for animals, as in humans, but also like humans, there are myriad other minor chakras located throughout the body.

Interestingly, an orange tomcat with whom I frequently work may have provided the answer to why men have nipples! I have learned through my work with him that the nipples are not merely ducts into the system of the mammary glands. They are also very receptive energy portals, and hand placement on an animal's belly during Reiki treatments has proven to boost the impact of the treatment.

As I work with Reiki energy, I know that healing will be directed to the areas where it is most needed. As Divine Source energy, it is intelligent and self-directing, and as such I do not believe that precise hand placement over the chakras is critical when doing animal work. Animals who are skittish of humans or in pain may have difficulty with being touched, and handling areas of fresh surgery or open wounds should be avoided to prevent infection.

Sometimes, when an animal settles down under my hands, we'll remain in the same position throughout the treatment.

Other times, animals will present me with the area that hurts, pushing their haunches or a sore ear against my hand. Still, it is valuable to understand the chakra system and be able to identify and focus intelligently on areas of difficulty for an animal.

Chakra is a Sanskrit word that means *wheel,* and this word is used to describe the spiraling motion of the energy the chakras contain. The seven major chakras, and the countless minor chakras, are centers for Ki (life force energy) to be gathered and distributed to the subtle and physical bodies. Each chakra corresponds to a layer of the auric field which surrounds the physical body; these layers are sometimes called the seven subtle bodies. Each chakra also provides energy for the physical body to remain vital and healthy.

Each chakra is associated with particular colors, crystals, plants, animals, astrological signs, musical notes, and essential oils with which it resonates. The chakras also directly affect and relate to every function of the body and mind. A brief overview of the chakras and their connections and correspondences, as is useful and relevant for working with animals, is given below.

- **The Crown Chakra:**

Location:	Just above the crown of the head
Associations:	Connection to Source, access to higher spiritual wisdom, Enlightenment, awareness of the Christ Consciousness
Auric field layer:	The Ketheric Template Body
Sanskrit:	Sahasrara – *a thousand-fold*
Element:	Universal Source
Color:	Violet and brilliant white
Crystals:	Clear quartz, selenite, spirit quartz

- **The Third Eye Chakra:**

Location:	The forehead, between the eyebrows
Associations:	Wisdom, intuition, thought processes, intellect, intuition, psychic vision and clairvoyance
Auric field layer:	The Celestial Body
Sanskrit:	Ajna – *to perceive*
Element:	The Cosmos
Color:	Indigo
Crystals:	Amethyst, iolite

- **The Throat Chakra:**

Location:	The throat
Associations:	The thyroid, throat, esophagus, communication, self-expression, the ability to communicate one's truth
Auric field layer:	The Etheric Template Body
Sanskrit:	Vishuddha – *purification*
Element:	Ether
Color:	Blue
Crystals:	Blue kyanite, apatite, lapis lazuli

- **The Heart Chakra:**

Location:	The chest, between the forelimbs, and also accessed between the shoulder blades on the back
Associations:	The heart, circulation, love of self and others, the center where the earthy and the celestial meet
Auric field layer:	The Astral Body
Sanskrit:	Anahata – *the unstruck*
Element:	Air

Color: Green and pink
Crystals: Rose quartz, chrysoprase,
                      rhodochrosite, peridot, green
                      calcite

- **The Solar Plexus Chakra:**
  Location: The upper abdomen between
                      the chest and the belly
  Associations: The primary sense of self, personal
                      power, the ability to command
                      one's circumstances, and confi-
                      dence to communicate one's truth
  Auric field layer: The Mental Body
  Sanskrit: Manipura – *lustrous jewel*
  Element: Fire
  Color: Yellow
  Crystals: Amber, citrine, sunstone, tiger's
                      eye, yellow calcite

- **The Sacral Chakra:**
  Location: The sacrum, roughly between the
                      hips
  Associations: The sexual organs, kidneys, blad-
                      ders, procreation, creativity,
                      relationships, emotions, self-worth,
                      feelings of deservedness, adaptabil-
                      ity, acceptance of change
  Auric field layer: The Emotional Body
  Sanskrit: Svadhistana – *your dwelling place,
                      your own sweet abode*
  Element: Water
  Color: Orange
  Crystals: Orange calcite, citrine, snowflake
                      obsidian

- **The Root Chakra:**

Location:	The base of the tail
Associations:	Hind legs, intestinal tract, defecation, grounding, connection to the Earth, security, stability, maintains the soul in a physical incarnation
Auric field layer:	The Etheric Body
Sanskrit:	Muladhara – *root or support*
Element:	Earth
Color:	Red or black
Crystals:	Black tourmaline, red jasper, black kyanite, aragonite

Animals and Color

An interesting discovery I have made in my animal Reiki work is that the color of an animal's fur can be an outward physical manifestation of areas of particular strength – and conversely the areas of greatest vulnerability – for that being. When learning to understand an animal's complaint and energetic make-up, I have come to take color into account. Here are some examples:

- **Black:** This is a classic color for the root chakra, and I have worked with a disproportionate number of black animals suffering from root chakra problems.

- A black cat who was nervous about being left alone in the house and suffered from separation anxiety, largely caused by a ghostly haunting which left her feeling vulnerable and unprotected.

- A black hound who was stricken with limb paralysis and had lingering issues with bowel control and hind-limb strength.

- A sweet black poodle mix with chronic hip and lower

back pain, a result of early-life injuries in his first home.

- A tricolored hound mix with a large black spot extending over his rump and tail afflicted with terrible fearfulness and insecurity which resulted in him over-guarding his home and biting a visitor.

- A black Schnauzer suffering deep-seated feelings of vulnerability, insecurity, and fear of humans after living as a homeless stray for some time. These feelings manifested as separation anxiety, defensive snapping, and restlessness.

- A black Coonhound mix with severe anxiety and panic disorders. After failing to thrive in two different homes, this dog was nervous and inconsistent in his behavior toward humans and dogs and was a Houdini at escaping confinement including leaping through two windows and destroying crates and kennels. He even tried to eat through a wall, tearing out electrical wiring and ripping out woodwork.

It is important to be open-minded when working with animals who display extreme or pronounced root chakra issues. In my sessions with the Houdini hound mentioned above, it became apparent that the dis-ease in the root center was a dramatic manifestation of heartbreak and wounding in the heart chakra. He needed heart-centered work, love energy, and emotional healing at a deep level before he was able to accept and process healing for anything else.

- **Orange:** The color of the sacral chakra, this color has also told me much about an animal's needs in terms of self image and relating to others.

I worked extensively with a beautiful orange cat who had difficulty with self-esteem and feelings of worthiness. Uncomfortable with himself and his unique characteristics, he needed reassurance to learn self-acceptance and find outlets to "be himself." He also had difficulty relating to people because he was concerned about being accepted for his unique self. His people made a concerted effort to celebrate his individuality, and this has helped him to feel special and valued just as he is.

The sacral chakra has much to do with how we engage in relationships. I worked with a big orange mixed-breed dog who had difficulty negotiating pack relationships in his family of animals. After a death in the family, he had felt the need to become the "protector male" but didn't know how to go about it.

It's very important for us to notice and consider how our animals relate to each other and to the humans in the family and social circle. I worked with a dog who mirrored her human's turmoil with another person by fighting with that person's dog. Animals often model patterns of human behavior – either positive or negative – and this can shed light on areas of human relationships and interpersonal skills that need improvement. This is one more way that both humans and animals are valuable teachers for each other, focusing with simplicity on even very complex issues.

- **Yellow:** This is the "power color" of the solar plexus chakra and can be indicative of an animal's level of self-empowerment.

Yellow animals I have known are extremely self-confident in exercising their personal power and asserting their will. They may be quick to make it known that their rightful place is at the center of the family, and they may be resistant to sharing toys or affection. Think of the lion and lioness in their personas of "King and Queen of the Jungle," and you will not be far off the mindset of a powerful yellow animal.

I worked with a yellow Labrador Retriever client who was emphatic about being the only animal in his family and felt himself to be the central member. While very giving and nurturing to his humans, he expected their loving devotion in return, knowing that he deserved it. With his masterful self-confidence, he fit naturally into his self-assigned role of chief masculine presence and guardian of the home.

A yellow Labrador whom I met at the shelter was rescued as a blind stray. The vulnerability and constant fear of being a blind dog living on the streets is about as far from "King of the Jungle" as you can get. He was in a condition of mind, body, and spirit that was the absolute antithesis of how such a dog is meant to be, and he required continual reassurance and bolstering of his confidence and worth.

The closest I have ever come to meeting the King of the Jungle was a long-haired yellow cat named Syd who had a hauntingly human face and very regal bearing. This cat was in quiet command everywhere he went – including into the backyards of other cats who were none too pleased. He was a self-aware observer, a quiet king of circumstance, and the emanations from his aura of power and harnessed ancient knowledge had a marked effect on those who came in contact with him.

Be aware of colors, their natural resonances with the various chakras, and the benefits of color therapy for animals. An energy healer can transmit colors into the animal's auric field during sessions. However, color therapy at home can be as simple as tying a bandana of a certain color around an animal's neck, choosing a particular color of blanket for his bed, or selecting crystals by color. If the root chakra needs assistance, red or black crystals will generally be beneficial, for example.

While there are no absolutes, color is another valuable tool to help us understand animals. Perhaps this is a form of expression which animals developed in order to compensate for the difficulty of communicating with humans. In any case, we need to be sure that we are attentive to all types of messages coming from animals.

Crystal Healing

rystal healing, which works with bioenergy fields, is another method of healing which illustrates how, at the metaphysical level, animals and humans are more similar than they are different. Most people believe that human beings possess a spirit, soul, eternal consciousness, or some sentient and intelligent aspect that remains intact and alive after the death of the body, and this is commonly regarded as energy, life force, or some other metaphysical component. As animals are also soul beings with complex energy systems, crystal work is as effective for them as for humans.

There are many veterinarians and healers who have worked with animal auras, chakras, and the totality of the animal energy system – and found it to be stunningly like ours. With this knowledge, it becomes more and more difficult to maintain the false notion that animals are not also spiritual. The naturally balanced resonances of crystals and minerals interact holistically with animals, addressing their spiritual aspects as well as mental, emotional and physical needs.

Many crystal healing regimens for animals are specifically tailored to work with emotions like love, security, self-confidence, grief, resentment, fear, and loneliness – the so-called "higher emotions" that some people erroneously believe are unique to humans. Other crystals have been found effective in working with animals at the soul level, elevating their spiritual well-being and assisting in the life-to-death transition. Again, as one delves deeper into the field of energy medicine, there come more insights into the spiritual nature of animals.

Crystals not only produce pyroelectricity and piezoelectricity (which were studied as early as the 6th century B.C. in Greece), crystals also produce, transmit, reflect, and focus electrical energy that merges with the electromagnetic field of the human or animal body. In *Hands-on Healing for Pets*, Margrit Coates states, "Biologists now know that in many cells of the body, both human and animal, there are living liquid crystals with subtle vibrations similar to those found in crystal stones. When we use crystal stones in healing, their vibrations link with the energy within the tissues of our pets." (p. 139, Coates, 2003)

More than just being comprised of crystalline forms, humans and animals are electrical beings, vibrating with an electromagnetic bioenergetic frequency at the molecular level. Animals, like humans, are permeated with and surrounded by energy fields. Natural crystal formations resonate with the energies of humans and animals in their physical and subtle bodies. It is also important to understand that many aspects of our environment can alter the form and function of the crystals and the energies within our bodies including music, plants, colors, and the subtle energy transmissions from the people and animals around us. (Scott and Mariani, 2002)

Unless the animal is already quite relaxed from a Reiki treatment or is ready for sleep, human treatment methods with crystals are largely impractical. For this reason, I do not recommend complex crystal grid layouts for direct-contact animal work. In my experience with dogs and cats, it would be difficult to convince an animal to lie still within a ring of stones for any length of time, let alone allow me to balance crystals on their backs from head to tail!

I generally only bring one crystal at a time to an animal session. I let the animals sniff and examine the crystal – while taking care that they don't swallow it. Sometimes, I'll hold the crystal in one hand while giving Reiki, or I may touch it against the animal's body over key chakra points. Some animals like to flop down on top of the crystal during a treatment, and this is another wonderful way that they accept its energy and healing vibration.

I have some large pieces of rose quartz engraved with the Usui Reiki symbols and charged with their energy. Rose quartz strengthens the heart energy on which Reiki travels, and these stones have been consecrated for Reiki healing. For a direct-contact session, I may lay these out in the room where the animal and I are working. I also place these stones in a circle around a picture of the animal in a distance session or sometimes place the stones around myself. I have found that this helps to focus and direct the energy to the recipient as well as strengthen its flow.

I tend to lay out very elaborate crystal grids around pictures of animals with whom I'm working in distance sessions, and I take care to consecrate and activate these grids for the highest benefit of the animal being served. Distance Reiki sessions are occasions when a variety of powerful crystals can be used in harmony with one another as the energy is directed remotely into the animal's field. A simple grid could include one stone for each chakra with some clear quartz to amplify the vibration. A more complex grid could include stones for invoking Angels and Guides or for assistance with specific issues like grief, depression, or healing from surgery.

A selenite wand used in distant healing sessions strengthens the Reiki bridge, the pure white light of the selenite energizing the connection. Pieces of selenite also serve to vitalize and activate crystal grids and can be used in conjunction with kyanite to hold a healing space and provide protective energy. Placing selenite lamps or towers near an animal's kennel or in places where he spends a lot time can help provide him with an energetic link to Spirit Guides and Angels.

Crystal wand massage is a wonderful technique for healing animals. This is really a massage of the subtle bodies rather than a physical body massage. A single-terminated crystal point or a specially-designed crystal wand with one pointed end and one rounded end work equally well.

The following two-step method of crystal wand massage I use is adapted from the technique described by Scott and Mariani in *Crystal Healing for Animals.*

1. Beginning over the root chakra and working up to the crown chakra, the practitioner holds the wand with the blunt end toward the animal and the pointed end up or out, moving the wand in a counterclockwise direction to remove negative energy.

   a. Where there are energetic plugs or any cords or collections of sickly energy, you will feel a drag on the wand as the crystal detects these structures. The wand will want to linger over a particular area until it is cleared. When the wand moves more easily and with a lighter feeling, it is time to progress to the next point on the body.

   b. Do not point the wand at yourself or others during this clearing and extraction process so as not to direct the negative energies into yourself or another.

   c. Use a particular process for sweeping away and grounding the energy you remove.

2. The process is then reversed. Beginning at the crown and moving to the root, the crystal point is towards the animal as the wand is moved in clockwise circles, channeling energy back into the chakra system.

   a. Again, you will feel the wand linger over areas that are in particular need of recharging and invigoration.

(Adapted from pp. 32-34, Scott and Mariani, 2002)

I have also used crystal wands as wicks to draw dark energy and blockages out of chakras. If you use this technique, you will become aware of the heavy, clogging structures being directed up through the crystal, and the wand should remain in place until the chakra is cleared. Depending on what has been removed, the wand may need to be cleared before reversing it to send positive energetic vibrations back into the chakra, or a second wand may need to be used if clearing the first is not practical during the treatment.

The following are my favorite wands to use with animals:

✓ Selenite for general detoxification and rejuvenation. Selenite brings a pure, white-light energy to treatment sessions and amplifies the healing properties of grids, layouts, and individual crystals. Selenite eliminates negative energies from the auric field and is an overall energetic tonic. This stone strengthens our energetic link with Source and helps us to access the highest level of spirituality and guidance.

✓ Bloodstone for older animals with kidney or liver problems or who take numerous medications.

✓ Lepidolite to aid with transition at the end of physical life.

✓ Rose quartz for emotional balance and stress relief.

✓ Blue kyanite is a bright crystal that resonates with all chakras and is particularly useful for animals with throat chakra issues or with whom you would like to deepen intuitive communication. Kyanite is a great chakra balancer and has the added benefit that it never needs clearing. I have also found it to be a very protective stone.

When working with crystal wanding, I sometimes place a large clear quartz crystal point on each side of the animal to amplify the healing effects of the wand. The presence of angelite is very useful when working with healing through Angelic helpers, and this crystal seems to harmonize well with the energies of every other stone with which I've combined it.

There are various techniques for dealing with the stagnant or negative energy being cleared, and it is important not to point the crystal wand toward the practitioner or anyone else during a removal. Some people ground the energy by directing it into the earth through various means like pointing fingers, intention, visualization, et cetera. You may use a visualization technique such as seeing the energy spiral down through the floor and into the Earth as you ask and intend for the Earth to receive and transmute it. You may work with the animal's Guardian Angels to carry the energy away and bring it to the light. I work with a Spirit Guide who gathers and removes dark or stagnant energies cleared during animal healing sessions, taking them to the Spiritual Realm for transmutation. I also work with the spirit of a wonderful river rock who accepts and holds negative energy until she can be set down on the Earth to release the energetic burden for transmutation.

Different sources suggest different crystals for similar purposes, and each practitioner has developed his or her crystals of choice for healing. In addition, usage guidelines for specific stones vary tremendously across sources. The choice of a crystal is very personal and individual to the healer and the needs of the client. I believe that if a healer develops a relationship with a particular stone and feels guided to use that stone, he or she should not feel limited or constrained by the recommendations given by a certain author or listed in a gemstone encyclopedia. The healer's loving intent to help is the single most important factor in making the healing effective.

Below is a sampling of my suggestions regarding crystals for animals:

✓ Amegreen: This is a fascinating combination of amethyst, prasiolite, and quartz and features beautiful purple, green, and crystal clear swirls and shadings. This is a gentle healing stone that stimulates compassionate love energy which combines with amethyst for heightened intuition. Amegreen links the heart center with the brow chakra, integrating love with clarity and insight. It is a bright all-around healer for illness or trauma, whether physical or emotional, and is both calming and soothing.

✓ Ametrine: This lovely stone is a combination of amethyst and citrine and is wonderful for creating harmony among human and animal family members when a new animal joins the home. This is a stone of balance and blending of opposites. Citrine has protective qualities while amethyst helps opens the user to higher guidance.

✓ Angelite: A pale blue stone, angelite is useful for invoking and attuning with the energy of Angelic healers. It also assists connection with an animal's Guardian Angels and helps both healer and animal to be open to Angelic communication. Overall, the vibration of angelite is very tranquil, and I find it to be a gentle stone.

✓ Aragonite: This is a beautiful stone with deep brown shadings on a golden background. It is an earthy stone and good for grounding and connecting to Mother Earth energies which help to dispel stress and feelings of in-security or restlessness. It is a centering stone which encourages peacefulness and acceptance.

✓ Black Tourmaline: A classic root chakra stone, black tourmaline is helpful for animals with insecurity or a lack of stability in their lives. It can help an animal who has been uprooted through abandonment or rehoming to feel connected and grounded on the Earth plane. Many animals suffering with hind leg, hip, and foot issues can benefit from the vibration of black tourmaline.

✓ Celestite: This watery blue stone is a wonderful crystal for Angel Healing. It assists in clarity of communication with the Angelic Realms and Spirit Guides and is also an aid to meditation.

✓ Citrine: This crystal is a classic choice for the solar plexus chakra. It has a bright, golden vibration which energizes and releases blockages. Citrine has protective qualities and never needs to be cleared, as it transmutes negative energies. When used in combination, it helps to keep other crystals clear. Its vibration also resonates with the crown chakra and facilitates spiritual access.

✓ Clear Quartz: This stone is a master healer of the Crystal Kingdom and its energies resonate with all chakras. Clear quartz is a powerful amplifier and director of energy and is particularly useful when combined with other crystals whose properties you want to boost. Quartz also holds energy received from a client or situation and needs to be cleared frequently and completely.

✓ Howlite: This soft, gentle white stone is very helpful for anxiety, depression, and dispelling negative energies and harmful emotions. Howlite clears and opens the user to higher guidance and energetic attunements.

✓ Lapis Lazuli: A beautiful throat chakra stone, lapis lazuli helps animals with self expression, boosting self-worth to enable an animal to speak his truth. Lapis also aids human-animal communication and opens one to receive greater levels of insight and information.

✓ Lepidolite: This is a mysterious, glittering, lavender stone which is a powerful helper for transitions of all kinds including moving, loss of a loved one, or re-homing. The vibration of lepidolite particularly brings comfort to dying animals and assists with the transition of the soul from life in Physical Reality to Light in the Spiritual Realm.

✓ Lithium quartz: This beautiful, lavender-tinted crystal combines the masterful healing properties of clear quartz with the anti-depressant nature of the naturally-occurring lithium which gives this quartz is color.

✓ Moonstone: Just as this is a stone of female empowerment for women, it also helps comfort pregnant female animals and assists with hormonal balancing in pregnancy and after giving birth. This stone is also said to help foster maternal bonding between a mother and her litter. A loving stone, moonstone helps humans to have a deeper understanding of animals.

✓ Orange calcite: This is a powerful stone for the sacral chakra and helps revitalize and clear the three lower chakras. It helps heal relationship issues and emotional problems and is also useful for promoting health of the reproductive system.

✓ Orange selenite: This crystal has the same properties as white selenite. It never needs clearing and works to clear and charge other crystals. It has a very pure vibration, and this color is good for calming turbulent energies in the sacral chakra and for ushering in clarity, peace, and protection.

✓ Peridot: This is a gentle green-gold stone that harmonizes the solar plexus chakra with the heart chakra. It helps particularly with self-acceptance and self-love in animals who have been abused and have suffered loss of identity and consequent feelings of being unlovable.

✓ Poppy Jasper: This stone is also called red brecciated jasper and is good for the root chakra. It is a wonderful grounding stone, activating Earth energies in the root chakra. Said to facilitate animal communication, poppy jasper is a relaxing stone that helps vitalize and detoxify the body.

✓ Rose Quartz: This a wonderful stone to open the heart and cleanse energy blockages caused by trauma, abuse, or neglect. Since Reiki is transmitted via the heart chakra of the practitioner, this stone helps to align the human with the animal client, and I have found that rose quartz can amplify the loving energy of a Reiki treatment. This is a wonderful stone for animals dealing with stress, abandonment, or any heartbreak.

✓ Selenite: In addition to crystal wanding (see above), it is matchless for empowering grids, creating protective energetic fields, and banishing negativity from the auric field and the chakras. It resonates with a pure white-light vibration and connects us with the Spirit Realm and the Divine. Its powerful energy is elevating to the soul and induces tranquility and peace. This crystal cannot hold negative energy and so never needs to be cleared. It also clears and recharges all other crystals and minerals. If you can only possess one crystal for healing, I suggest selenite. A note of caution: It should never get wet as this will damage the crystal. It scratches and mars easily, so take care to protect it.

✓ Snowflake obsidian: Like black tourmaline, this is a good grounding stone. It is also good for the sacral chakra. Snowflake obsidian helps to release painful emotional blockages and clears negative energies. This is a stone of protection and helps to foster tranquility and emotional calm.

✓ Tiger's Eye: This earthy stone seems to carry with it an energetic touch of Archangel Ariel. It is a wonderful stone for the solar plexus chakra and helps animals deal with issues of personal sovereignty, dignity, and personal expression and power.

The following are some crystal combinations I have found effective when secured in bags and placed safely in the animal's living area or for grids and use on the body:

✓ Orange calcite, citrine, poppy jasper, and clear quartz. These were helpful for Maxwell, a shelter cat who had severe skin allergies, a nervous condition, and self-worth problems. (When another cat at the shelter started sleeping in Maxwell's bed to draw energy from his  crystals, I was asked to bring a set for her as well)!

✓ Snowflake obsidian, rose quartz, citrine, amegreen, and selenite. This was a nice combination for a contented, 14-year-old cat with some age-related health problems. She appreciates crystal energy, and these crystals provided a gentle, bright vibration for her. White selenite in the mix also served to keep the rest of the crystals clear and charged.

✓ Clear quartz, rose quartz, aragonite, and orange selenite. I chose this combination for a very fearful, anxious dog. I wanted to combine gentle, supportive energy for the heart chakra with grounding and calming vibrations. The clear quartz amplifies the vibrations of the other crystals, and the selenite serves a dual purpose of keeping the crystals cleared and charged as well as emitting its own healing vibration.

✓ Black tourmaline and red jasper. This is a wonderful, classic combination of stones for the root chakra. These work superbly for grounding and helping with all root chakra complaints such as insecurity, gait problems, et cetera.

✓ Citrine and golden tiger's eye. These complement each other for working with the solar plexus chakra and issues of personal power, self-esteem, and self-worth. Tiger's eye in particular carries the energy of Archangel Ariel and is helpful for animals in all circumstances, particularly when combined with the bright, cleansing vibration of golden citrine.

A note on clearing crystals: It is essential to clear crystals when you obtain them and after any use for healing, even in distance treatments. Crystals like quartz not only absorb energy, they amplify it, so any negative energy which has come into the quartz from a session will be sent out many-fold to those who use the crystal afterwards without clearing it. Most other crystals also absorb negativity.

• Clear your crystals when you first get them by holding them under cold running water and then laying them out in the sun (on a windowsill, deck, or on the Earth) to recharge.

• Another way to clear crystals is to soak them in cool salt water for 10-15 minutes; I like to use sea salt for this. Be sure to rinse them off afterwards and set in sunlight or moonlight to recharge. (Salt extracts which makes it good for clearing. Cool running water disrupts etheric patterns).

• Smudging with sage or a clearing and protective incense like cedar is also quite effective.

Selenite cannot be gotten wet as it is very soft and will dissolve. Selenite also never needs to be cleared as it cannot hold negative energies. If you have a large piece of selenite, you can lay your crystals on it to clear and recharge them (my favorite way).

Do not wet any Himalayan salt lamps or crystals as they will dissolve.

Do not place amethyst, ametrine, or fluorite in direct sunlight as this can fade the color. Use moonlight instead.

The crystals that I feel confident do not absorb negativity and do not need clearing are:

- Citrine
- Kyanite (all colors)
- Salt
- Selenite (all colors)

As you work with your crystals, you will get to know their vibrations and become attuned to their uses. You will even receive intuitive information on which crystals are best-suited for a particular situation. Interact with the spirits of the crystals and minerals, invoking their help in your healing work, and create a way to consecrate them for healing. If you have been attuned to Reiki, you can charge your crystals with Reiki energy to boost their healing properties.

Treat your crystals as the prized healing partners they are, and store them with care. I do not display my healing crystals as I want to keep them energetically pure between uses. I keep them in sealed and labeled boxes inside a beautiful, glass-fronted case that my husband made for this purpose. My crystal case holds a fitting place of honor in my treatment room.

Below is a crystal grid I designed for a distance Crystal Reiki session designed to bring harmony to a family of dogs experiencing discord. This grid featured a lot of rose quartz for its loving heart chakra vibration, ametrine to foster harmony, angelite and celestite to invoke assistance from the Angelic Realms, black tourmaline to bolster the root chakra, and silver topaz to strengthen the energy transmission.

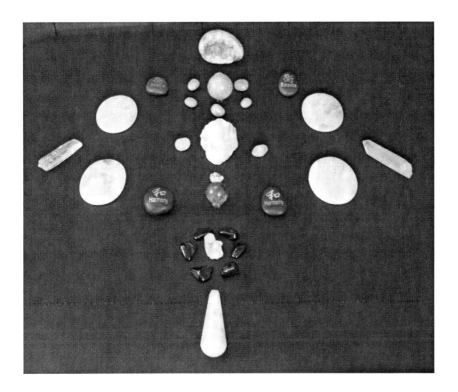

Caution: What Animal Energy Work Does *Not* Do

In *Animal Reiki*, the authors caution that Reiki provides healing to an animal "within the framework of that being's destiny" and that, while Reiki can improve the quality of life for a terminally ill animal and make his transition easier (as well as assisting his family members), "...healing doesn't always mean cure." (pp. 154-155, Fulton and Prasad, 2006) I would go on to add from my experience that healing is accepted and integrated by an animal according to his free will, truest desires, and highest good. As in the case of Buster which I recounted earlier, that sometimes means letting go of the physical body, even if this is not in alignment with the wishes of the animal's loved ones.

Reiki and other forms of healing compliment but should not substitute for medical care by a veterinarian. This is consistent with my Reiki training that all maladies filter down to the physical body due to dis-ease somewhere in the subtle energy bodies. Just as Reiki and other Lightworkers are needed to address the energetic root causes of illness, a veterinarian is needed to assist in dealing with the physical ramifications which have appeared. Lightworkers do not diagnose or prescribe treatment for physical medical problems but instead are concerned with energy. A veterinarian should always be consulted for concerns about an animal's health, behavior, or wellbeing.

Vibrational healing is not a magic pill for behavioral problems in animals. For example, Reiki helped Jack to recover from trauma and depression. However, it did not alter Reggie's frantic barking and overstimulation anxiety in the car; rather it facilitated a connection with me whereby he could ask for help and say, "Make me less nervous." A dog who doesn't get enough exercise, spends all his time alone, or is fed a poor diet high in sugars is going to experience the repercussions, whether he receives Reiki or not.

A puppy mill dog with whom I worked showed me a scene from her life in a bleak outdoor shed filled with stacked rows of wire cages, wooden boards beneath them splattered with urine and excrement. For eight years, she gave birth on wire, nursed puppies in squalor, and lived in fear. Holding her close to my body and giving Reiki allowed her to process and release some of her anguish and provided loving comfort and her first-ever channel of communication with a human being. However, the most critical step for this dog had been getting her out of the puppy mill and into the rescue shelter. Reiki came later.

Animal communicators and psychic mediums are not "mind readers." We can only relate what the animal is willing to share with us. We also are not sorceresses or wizards who can "make" an animal behave in a desired way.

No one can force another being to do anything if it is against his or her will. Besides this, zeroing in on the animal's "problem behavior" is not always the correct focus. There are usually broader underlying problems involving people, other animals, medical issues, or past abuse. An animal's life must be looked at holistically including family members, home environment, diet, exercise, training methods, mental stimulation, and physical health.

A complete animal care team includes an animal energy worker, veterinarian, behaviorist/trainer, and family members. Caring for an animal is a lifelong commitment, and animals have their ups and downs just as people do, although it takes more initiative and effort to sort them out. It may not be readily apparent if a cat's inappropriate urination around the house is from resentment or a bladder infection, or if a dog's sudden biting is from a painful medical problem or a case of anxiety. Your veterinarian and other professionals can help steer you through these sometimes murky waters as together you seek the best outcome for your animal companion.

Animals as Healers

In her groundbreaking book, *Essential Reiki*, Reiki Master Diane Stein states, "The act of laying hands on the human or animal body to comfort and relieve pain is as old as instinct," adding, "When an animal is in pain, a dog or cat's first instinct is to lick the pain area – for the same reasons that a person applies touch with her hands. An animal mother will also lick her young in distress. This simple act is the basis for all touch healing techniques." (p. 16, Stein, 1995) Here, Stein is not only including animals amongst potential *receivers* of Reiki, but also as active *channelers* of healing energy, suggesting a healing partnership among species.

Before studying Reiki, I had intuitively or instinctively *known* how to do hands-on healing. I have met other healers who also felt they had innate knowledge of hands-on touch work prior to any formal training. Some Reiki Masters believe that all Reiki training in this lifetime is a remembering of what we have done as Reiki practitioners in past lifetimes. I would go further and say that all soul beings on the Earth have an innate knowledge of vibrational medicine and healing touch work.

All species of animals use some form of touch to soothe and express concern. Our animal companions love and comfort us and other animals physically and energetically, sending us loving energy and helping our bodies to release endorphins that aid in healing and feelings of peace. I am routinely nurtured by my 75-pound lapdog, Reggie, who makes it his mission to watch over me when I am unwell by guarding my body, offering kisses, and assiduously licking every tear from my face. He is frantic to reach me with consoling kisses if he hears even the faintest tone of distress in my voice.

I spent an afternoon one Saturday at a "holistic healing expo" that was filled with psychic mediums, astrologers, chiropractors, shamans, shop owners, angel readers, intuitives, and others. In an overheated hotel conference room, they jockeyed for position, the clear and soft light of the Spirit Guides and the Angels and even the Reiki completely overwhelmed by the harsh glare of commercialism.

It could have been any sort of business convention. With so many Lightworkers gathered together, I expected wonderful, healing, enlightened energy to be flying around like stardust. Instead, it was a collection of tired people who had devoted a substantial portion of their lives to alternative healing, Eastern religion, channeling, or other disciplines and were trying to scratch a living in a society that frequently doesn't care or doesn't even know what they do or why it matters.

I saw the cliques, the "in crowd" and the "out crowd." I stood on the edge of conversations where I wasn't quite welcome. I handed out flyers for a class I was teaching and was regarded with suspicion. I felt the insecurities, the competitiveness, and even thinly veiled hostility. All this was amplified by the tables full of quartz crystals to create a veritable smog of negativity.

Coming home to my three dogs was one of the biggest energetic shocks I've ever had. Out of a dark storm of toxic energy, I walked into a realm of harmonious, loving, life-affirming peace. And yes, it was indeed peace I felt, even with paws slapping down on my shoulders as Reggie climbed up my body to kiss me and Jack and Oscar crowded in on either side. It was warm, genuine love and welcome without guile, or manipulation, or anything required other than that I merely exist. It is this unstinting honesty in an environment of emotional safety that leads us to a place of clarity where our inner wisdom can prevail.

Sitting in the sun in my Adirondack chair with a dog in my lap, I asked why my day had been so rotten, why I had felt so vulnerable and abraded and was so inexplicably near to tears. *Because your heart is pierced* came the soft answer. Who then could mend it? I asked Archangel Michael for his help, but he only said that I must go down into the Earth to heal. This was a mending that needed rock and sky, soil and grass and trees – and animals.

We humans have become strangers, aliens in the very landscape in which we need to enfold ourselves to find healing and abundant life. Animals are our guides and our teachers. In their knowing of the deep things of the world, animals hold the keys to all the doors that have shut in our faces. We need them. We rely on them.

The loving attitude of animals helps us to soften our harsh and unloving judgments of both ourselves and others. When we feel angry or sad and unlovable, the kisses of dogs and cats provide comfort and reassurance – and when they extend this same generosity of heart to someone with whom we've been quarreling, they shine a light on the loving core of the other person, the *real* person to whom they're responding, and they facilitate peacemaking and fence mending. Our companion animals perceive the best in us and are a lens through which we can see the higher potential of other people. We feel safe allowing the animals to access vulnerable parts of our make-up which we protect from intrusion by humans.

The mere presence of animals can be a balm to an aching soul. I learned this from my sweet dog Jack in a very poignant way in 2009. At the end of January that year, my father was in hospice care, his physical body overwhelmed by congestive heart failure which had led to kidney and liver shut-down. Daddy had always been the center of the family. It was an agonizingly painful time as he lived through his last days and we each tried to steel ourselves for the final physical parting.

As I went through the motions, trying to carry on with work

and the tasks of daily life, I browsed through various animal rescue shelter websites as I always did, looking at the pictures and
reading the stories of dogs, cats, and other creatures who had
fallen on hard times. Something indefinable about Jack leapt out
at me.

I returned to his picture again and again over the next few
days until I was seized with an inexplicable, burning desire to
rush to the shelter and adopt him, sight unseen. I was so nervous
that I had wasted precious days and had lost my chance, I asked
a friend to call the animal shelter and see if he was still available.
He was – but they added that he'd been featured for adoption on
a television spot that day. I swung into high gear.

Heart pounding, I called my husband and explained that we
had to adopt Jack. I didn't know why – we just did. I asked him
to go across town to the doggie daycare and collect Reggie, our
18-month-old pointer, and then meet me in the parking lot of my
office building. There was no time to lose! I told all my cowork-
ers I was adopting another dog and arranged to leave early for
this out-of-the-blue, high-stakes mission.

God love him, my husband Ben never blinked. He used to
say that, "One animal is all we can handle." I asked him why he
was so willing to meet this dog, why he was going along with
me – and he couldn't explain it, saying only that "This time is
different" and "It just seems right."

We marched into the shelter with Reggie in tow, and the
woman who met us thought we were there to abandon him!
She was quite shocked when I produced an incredibly homely
picture of Jack from the Internet and announced, "We want to
meet this dog. We were told the adoption would go faster if we
brought our other dog."

Jack and I met alone in a tiny, cell-like introduction room.
He was shy and suffering from a head cold, wearing a shabby
secondhand collar that didn't fit, and wondering where he was
going next. I asked him, "Do you want me to be your Mommy?

Do you want to come home and be my little boy?" Scared, dirty, his tail between his legs, he gave me his answer. I brought him out to meet the rest of the family, and Ben announced, "Well, I'm ready to adopt him now."

We wanted to pick him up the next day after we'd had a chance to buy bowls, toys, a Gentle Leader, and a name tag but were firmly told that they needed the kennel space and couldn't hold him. I scrambled around a closed retail shop, buying a Gentle Leader and a rubber bone and whatever else I could grab – and Jack walked into the house that night, 24 hours to the very minute before my father passed away.

The night that Daddy died, I was sobbing in our bed and told Ben that I "wanted everyone with me." He and the dogs lay down with me, surrounding me like a living wall of love and support, and Jack  spent his first-ever night in a real bed. In the days and nights that followed, with Jack's gentle presence, my grief was easier to bear. The work and excitement and love of having a new dog-child in the house was healing and helped me carry on when my heart was at its most raw.

I knew that an Angel had whispered in my ear on that January day, "Go and get Jack and bring him home." In rescuing him, I had rescued a part of myself. A long while later, a psychic medium relayed a message from my father, that he had been the one who led us to Jack because he wanted me to have more love in my life at the time when he knew he would be leaving us. While traveling outside his body near death, he had come upon Jack and heard his longing prayer for love – and in a final earthly act as a devoted father, Daddy brought love to all of us.

Another story of healing I've been asked to share is that of a woman whose dog rescued her from her darkest hours. She had become severely depressed to the point of contemplating suicide, feeling deeply alone despite the presence of concerned family and friends. One particularly bleak afternoon, she climbed down the banks of a deep river and stood at the water's edge, preparing to drown herself.

Her young dog came down to stand beside her, surveying the water that she envisioned as her grave. Direct from his heart came a shaft of love so deep and so penetrating, he wordlessly restored her will to live. She turned back, she said, because of him.

She successfully obtained medical help for her depression and credits her dog with the fact that she's alive and well today. "He needed me and loved me with a purity of heart that no one else had. He brought a ray of hope into my darkness that led me to seek help before it was too late."

A man named Shawn also described to me this wordless and profound spiritual connection with an animal. "My family had a terrier named Kokomo, and we would always make eye contact and stare into each other's eyes with intimacy. I knew he loved me, and he knew I loved him, and he had the most beautiful rusty brown eyes."

They are so well-suited, these creatures, to bring succor to our hearts and souls. It is that very "purity of heart," the confidence "I knew he loved me," and the soul-level intimacy with their humans that makes this healing possible.

One of the most impressive lessons that animals can teach humans is that we should each be true to our essential nature as beings. Dogs persist in being dogs and do not act like cats even if feline traits are held in higher esteem at some moment in time. If a wolf pack fails to outflank the mule deer they had chosen, they will hunt again according to their given talents and will eventually be successful.

Ted Andrews states, "What blocks most people from manifesting their dreams in life is their fear of being who they are." (p. 33, Andrews, 1993) He points out that animals do not waste their energies on manufacturing pointless fears. Because animals behave according to who and what they are, they are able to recognize and then capitalize upon essential opportunities. Animals put forth efforts in accordance with their innate abilities and characteristics and do not persist in processes that are unsuccessful. Animals "never get hung up on fruitless repetition of behaviors and patterns that are doomed to fail." (p. 34, Andrews, 1993)

Through observing the animals who make themselves known in our lives and learning to discern their messages, we can learn much about how to live and act in ways geared for success. A barn owl knows that his keen sight and soundless wings give him an advantage over a mouse. Therefore, he chooses to hunt mice by such methods, and he thrives. He has no illusion of being in a position to compete with a grizzly bear hunting for salmon in rushing rapids. However, the owl does not see himself as diminished because of this. He sees himself as exceptionally talented and powerful in the sphere to which he is innately suited.

Many people have experienced animal healing through profound spiritual connections. In my healing work with animals, I have become aware of what I sometimes call Animal Spirit Guides who assist me in my practice. One such Guide is Buster who helps other dog souls in their transition processes. Another is a cat spirit I call Jasmine, who was seen by a healer curled up on my belly during a Reiki session I received, a spirit who made her presence known at a time when I was facing challenges with cat clients at the shelter. Still another is Wally, a Mastiff mix who passed away before I came to the shelter but whose story is what compelled me to begin work there; I sense his presence as a Guardian Spirit at the shelter and have seen his energy near an animal caregiver who is still grieving for him.

The most compelling accounts of animals as spiritual healers come from shamanic beliefs and practices. The following information is derived from an interview I conducted with practicing shaman Alan Jacobs. He has trained extensively with shamanic teachers all across the United States and practices shamanic healing at a crisis center for sexual abuse victims, leads journeying circles, and provides healing and insight to clients in his private shamanic practice.

Shamanism is the oldest spiritual practice among humans and developed globally in various forms. Scholars have demonstrated evidence of shamanic practices dating back at least 60,000 years. For the shaman, all of life on earth is inextricably woven together, and all things embody spirit – humans, animals, plants, rocks, water, et cetera. Whereas there is a hierarchy among creatures on Earth as regards mission, purpose, and place on the food chain, this hierarchy is relegated to the physical world only. The spirits or souls of all beings are seen to be equal and of the same substance.

For the shaman, recognizing and maintaining connectedness to Source and to all of life is paramount. Animals are seen as interconnected with humans in the web of life, spirits who chose to embody animal forms for the fulfillment of specific missions and functions, much like sprits that chose to incarnate in human forms. A very important and complex animal spirit for the shaman is the Power Animal.

According to Alan Jacobs, a Power Animal is a spirit being who volunteers to protect and assist humans from the time of infancy. A child without at least one Power Animal helper is regarded as unable to survive the trials and tribulations of

human development and maturation. The Power Animal may take the form of virtually any animal, and no animal form is felt to be more or less significant or potent than any other. What is important is that the Power Animal embodies traits and characteristics that the person needs in order to live effectively as a balanced and productive individual. One such example was a monkey spirit returning a sense of playfulness and energy to a man who felt lethargic and depleted.

Power Animals may come and go, bringing gifts that are needed temporarily to assist with a given problem. Power Animals can also be driven away through lack of acceptance or by disrespect, leaving a person with low energy, open to spiritual attack, and lacking certain skills needed for his or her life challenges. In that case, a shaman may assist with a Power Animal retrieval which is carried out through a journeying process in which the shaman moves among different layers of reality to interact with spirits. An individual may also directly seek out his or her Power Animal through journeying.

Power Animals also serve as critical healing partners in the shaman's work. Alan Jacobs works with an array of Power Animals, each with a particular unique function such as transporting the shaman between levels of reality, assisting with spiritual healing, work in water, or ego work. Alan described that as a shaman he merges at a metaphysical level with a partic-

OTHER NATIONS

ular Power Animal to perform diagnostic scans of patients and other healing work, literally looking out of the Power Animal's eyes and using the Power Animal's heightened senses and advanced spiritual abilities.

Different indigenous cultures have developed different concepts regarding the precise nature of Power Animals and their interactions with humans. Some shamanic belief systems assert that a Power Animal is the spirit/soul of an animal that lived in that physical form on the Earth plane and has chosen to return in spirit form, still embodying the characteristics of the animal, in order to assist humans in their survival and development. Some other groups see Power Animals more as protective guides. Still other shamanic systems believe that by ingesting the organs of an animal – for example the heart or the eyes – the animal's characteristics such as courage or far-reaching sensory acuity are made available to a human. What is common across all shamanic systems, however, is that the Power Animal has a true connection to the person.

Animal behaviorist and counselor Diana L. Guerrero has also studied the role of animals in the spiritual lives of indigenous peoples and ancient cultures. She states that folklore of many countries is replete with accounts of shape-shifting – or transmutation of a person into animal form, merging with an animal to take on the creature's characteristics. She adds, "Although some people consider these stories and practices to be primitive or silly, they are actually important lessons about how we can practice shifting our energies to meet the daily challenges of life." (p. 115, Guerrero, 2003)

Very much aligned with the shamanic concept of the Power Animal, each god and goddess in the vast Hindu pantheon has an animal vehicle which represents the animal attributes and energies which we, in our human form, need either to enhance or moderate with the help of their associated deities. Study your Power Animals and the animals who increasingly make themselves known in your life, and then learn about the deities associated with them to see which spiritual beings may be reaching out to assist you in some area of your life. Some examples of gods and goddesses and their animal vehicles are Ganesha and the mouse, Brahma and the swan, Lakshmi and the owl, and Ganga and the crocodile.

I regard the Power Animal as synonymous with the Totem Animal which to me is an animal who presents to a person in both physical and spirit form for the teaching of powerful lessons representative of the highest level of ability and understanding of the collective members of that Clan (or group of animals which are represented by the Totem). The unique wisdom and characteristics innate to that particular species is the Totem Animal's medicine.

For example, a very shy person whom I know recounted a journey filled with wolves. The wolf medicine that this person needed was to learn assertiveness with self-control, to find personal strength through working in a group (akin to the wolf pack), and to understand how the predation process in Nature both gives and takes. This give-and-take of the wolf-hunter illustrated that seeking what one wants or requires need not be an unbalanced, selfish endeavor that takes advantage of others. Wolf encouraged him to step into his power with the confidence that this could be moderated by self-discipline.

My first encounter with a Power Animal was during a shamanic journey that I undertook with the guidance of Alan Jacobs at a time when I was seeking higher-level wisdom because my husband and I were being victimized by an unscrupulous building contractor who severely damaged our home. I met with a tiger who laid down with me and on me and then opened his mouth, growling and displaying his teeth, apparently attacking me. I forcibly fended off the tiger, and then found myself merging with him. He was not attacking me but was teaching me a lesson about my anger. I needed to guard against the ferocity of my rage devouring me, and instead of the fierceness and aggression of the tiger, I needed to adopt his other qualities: Watchfulness, alertness, keen senses, grace, controlled strength. I actually felt my hands as the tiger's paws and claws as I fully embodied him, and then there was a gentle separation when I was recalled from the journey.

On subsequent journeys, I have encountered birds of many kinds. When I was seeking my teacher, I rode a barge through tunnels of rock, and numerous birds got onto the barge with me – cockatiels, parrots, and others. Several times, an owl has brought me to my destinations and then returned for me when it was time to depart.

Numerous physical and metaphysical experiences with owls have highlighted my affinity for working with owl medicine and my powerful connection to this animal. I had a series of childhood dreams of a white owl who appeared at intervals to impart wisdom and instruction. In Arizona when I was about seven, my father and I came upon an enormous white owl in the shrubbery beside my bedroom that took off in glorious flight into the east. Engaged by their qualities of magic, I have always sought the company of owls and have had mystical experiences in their presence.

For several months while writing this book, I was visited every day by a loudly hooting owl at precisely 2:00 p.m. – not prime time for a nocturnal creature. When we sprang forward into daylight savings time, the visits continued unabated, only at 3:00 p.m. I asked what message owl had come to convey and realized that I was being reminded to use my owl vision daily, to see with the "Eye of Horus" for effective manifestation on the physical plane. In the midst of a busy life, this is a very useful daily reminder to all of us to take time and concentrate on our abilities of co-creation.

Reiki Master Victoria Swanson described a beautiful Bengal tiger pacing back and forth around me, a protective guardian.

Indeed I had already met this tiger whom she saw, the Power Animal mentioned before who had come to me in a time of need. She has also seen me surrounded by a whole company of animal spirits including an eagle, a condor, a domesticated housecat, and many others whom she recognizes as my helpers; always, she says, there is an owl with me.

Power Animals are enormous contributors to all forms of energy work. At a Reiki share evening, I was performing a group session with another practitioner and became powerfully aware of two polar bears who showed themselves striding through snows in the thin atmosphere and pale skies of the Arctic Circle. When I asked if any of the others saw these spirits, the client on the table laughed and said, "Well, I'm in the arms of a polar bear right now!" referring to the primary Totem Animal of the other practitioner, Robbie. I learned that she even owns a business called White Bear Ways. Later, when I was on the Reiki table and Robbie placed her hands on me, I immediately saw snowy owls, and she shared that this is another of her Totems and that she has images of white owls all over her house.

Whether as vehicles of the gods as in the Hindu tradition, benevolent helper spirits of the Buddhist Goddess of Compassion Kwan Yin, or the little brothers and sisters to whom St. Francis of Assisi preached the Gospel of Jesus, animals have been precious to many religious and spiritual traditions throughout the ages. Be watchful for what animals appear in your life – on television, in the park, or in your living room. These soul beings have messages for you that can help empower your life.

I once read a moving passage about a blue heron in the excellent Civil War novel *Cold Mountain* by Charles Frazier – and saw a blue heron for the very first time beside a wooded creek the next day. A Great Blue Heron then appeared to me in a meditation for a metaphysical class about symbols and became a topic of conversation when friends and I saw a flight of these majestic birds cross a farm field. Apparently, the heron is very persistent in being noticed! I learned that this beautiful bird is actually my personal symbol, representing the ability to move forward gracefully with self-determination and independence of spirit.

The animals truly are speaking. It is our function to open up and listen. When you learn to hear and internalize their wisdom, you will be amazed at the transformative power of their messages. This is power all of us have always possessed but rarely use in the modern world. Begin working with it now and discover all the animal guides and helpers who will come to you along the way.

Animal Meditations

The process of entering into meditation to merge with animals is an old shamanic practice taught by Alan Jacobs and other contemporary shamans who guide journeyers to meet with Power Animals. This has been adopted by animal communicators and healers such as Margrit Coates and Karen Craft who both advocate this technique for deepening understanding of and connection to animals.

There are numerous books and resources available detailing the metaphysical qualities of many species. These are my findings, drawn from my personal mystical experiences with the spirits of animals.

Birds

Blue Heron: The blue heron's curving neck and long legs epitomize the one who moves through life with balletic grace. A loner, this bird is a free spirit who rises above the mundane trials and tribulations of the world. Habituating riverbanks and other watersides, she moves seamlessly from one realm to the next – air, land, water – bridging them all with masterful ease. If blue heron is your totem, you may find yourself most at home in places and in situations that are in between black-and-white exactitude – particularly if the locale or circumstance is fashioned according to your own design. Take time for contemplation and self-reflection, and then move forward with determination. Individualism, independence, muscular grace, ease of movement – all describe the attributes of the Great Blue Heron.

Gull: The seagull who alights on the railing at a wharf-side café to snap up tidbits of fish is more than a casual observer of the human diners whose food he shares. Birds are masters of the sky, riders of the air and attuned to its currents. As these are much like the eddying currents of time, birds travel telepathically forward and backwards along the time continuum. If you lock gazes with a gull and your heart is open, he may see much of your past as it flows into the distance – as well as your future course along the current of time on which you ride.

Owl: The owl is perhaps the most spiritual of birds. I have met with owl Spirit Guides in dreams, shamanic journeys, and healing sessions as well as in physicality. Indeed, I have a Guardian Angel who has the wings of an owl.

Owls see in the darkness. A great lesson in owl-sight has been seeing the soul nature of animals and resonating with the great truth that we share spiritual Oneness with all forms. Another has been the use of our inner vision to consciously co-create.

Owl teaches that victory belongs to the watchful and the swift. When you perceive that your goal is within reach, swoop down and seize it. Be alert for opportunity and launch a timely strike when it appears – lest like the mouse or the hare, the elusive chance will return to the shadows of the tall grass and be lost.

Swan: These water fowl are the chariots of angels and the purveyors of dreams. Guardian Angels sometimes travel in swan-shaped boats as they navigate the dark and sinister waters of human troubles. Swans are also great journeyers, flying dream travelers upon their backs.

Swans make life look easy – smooth and graceful on top but with a lot of swift paddling underneath. There are even some swans who paddle with only one foot in order to change direction swiftly when needed. Swan medicine teaches that hard work pays off when you glide elegantly to the finish, but nothing of stature comes effortlessly. Do your work behind the scenes to get what you want.

Building their nests on the water's edge, swans know their domain of power and don't stray far from it. Indeed, many swans nest where they themselves hatched or where nesting and rearing of cygnets has been successful in the past. Swans mate for life and have strong family bonds, and they represent fidelity and partnership.

Canines

Dog: Dogs are a true embodiment of unconditional love, reflecting in their expressive eyes a depth of devotion and loyalty that is otherworldly. Indeed, the love of a dog comes from a better and a higher world, from the Divine Realm, and reflects the Agape love of God into our flawed and sometimes bleak land of physicality. For anyone who has attracted dogs as Power Animals or as companions, be grateful for the blessing of their presence in your life.

Dogs love boundlessly, endlessly as they seek the filial company of other beings with whom to share their affection and their lives. These sweet and noble animals teach us the importance of our social groups and that loving others can be worth the risk. In the face of cruel and unjust punishment, abandonment, and betrayal, dogs never lose hope that somewhere is a human worthy of their love and faithfulness. So we too must not lose our belief in humanity and in the other inhabitants of the Earth. By holding out hope for their Enlightenment and softened hearts, we create the possibility for the unfoldment of human consciousness and the elevation of our species.

If you are privileged to love a dog, you know how he strengthens and uplifts you even in your darkest hours. He asks for no return but your loving presence – and even if that is withheld from him, he will continue to hope for it and to hold out another chance for you to live up to his expectations. The signature of dog medicine is love laced with hope, forgiveness, and the willingness to hold out a hand of friendship to others.

Wolf: When this hunter sinks his teeth into the soft throat of a deer, there is no doubt that he has reveled in the hunt and in the victory of his catch. One of many ways this grand creature differs from the human predator is his awareness of the spirit of his prey as it passes into the ethers. Even as her warm blood flows into his mouth, the wolf watches as the doe's spirit hovers briefly in the glade, and he acknowledges this, knowing it for the Divine spark that it is. He honors the cycle of life through this seeing and knowing of the spirits in all things. The kill shall be used wisely and with the greatest efficacy.

Strong and courageous, wolves are not loners. They have learned to magnify their individual strength through multiplicity in the pack. These canines know how to live and work in social groups, asserting themselves when necessary but also yielding and showing respect for others. Wolves teach the lesson of strength in numbers and the natural unity of the pack – which in turn points us to the true Unity of all beings.

Cetaceans

A Word About the Seas: In meditation, I was taken to see a great figure like Buddha or Krishna suspended above a quiet bay, surrounded by slowly rotating rings of lighted candles. Many dolphins swam beneath him in the brilliant moonlit water. When I asked his name, he called himself The Teacher of the Eternal Sea. The future of mankind, he said, lies in the oceans.

He counseled that no human should eat the flesh of any beast

or fish, but freely-given milk (and by extension cheese and but-
ter) were acceptable. He taught that people should consume only
plants that could be sustainably grown and harvested. This diet,
he said, would purify the body and the mind and enable greater
flights of meditation and deeper journeying states in which we
could be schooled in wisdom.

This Teacher warned against overfishing and anything that
damages the ecosystems of the oceans. Commercial fishing and
whaling were shown to be having particularly harmful effects.
To this, I would add a cautionary statement against the slaughter of seals, offshore oil drilling, and activities that pollute our
waterways and seas.

If the future of mankind lies in the oceans, we would do well
to study our oceanic past as well. The vanished civilization of
Atlantis was a culture of great spiritual freedom. Atlanteans harnessed Earth energies, such as those of the Crystal and Mineral
Kingdoms, for healing and as clean energy sources. The people
of Atlantis also respected and communed with the great wisdom
keepers of the deeps, the dolphins and whales, and lived with
them in peace.

The power of the Divine Feminine was not a thing to be
feared in Atlantis, but water, the most feminine of the elements,
was prized and harmonized with the masculine element of the
air. As the Divine Feminine energies are reemerging now to
return harmonic balance to the Universe, it is truly a hope to
cherish that our future as seafarers and sea-sharers might herald
a return to an even higher and more lasting Atlantean revival.

Dolphin: The beings now incarnated as dolphins are very
highly-developed spiritual entities. They chose their currently
earthly form of existence precisely because it is more elevated
and evolved than other forms. Dolphins are great telepaths and
welcome communication with humans.

Eliad is a dolphin who linked with me telepathically to convey an image of the heavens opening and releasing a bright waterfall beneath a brilliant moon, this great surge washing blood from the water. Her message: The world is changing. Humans are like wooden statues or chess pieces, bound by our need for money and our obsession with the objects we make. The dolphins are truly free. Nature has created all that they need or desire, and they are free to concentrate on Spirit, a purer existence, and higher planes. To free ourselves, humans must shift our focus to Spirit and teaching of the Spirit.

<u>Whales</u>: Whales are the Watchers, the Sentinels of this planet. The health of the Earth is mirrored in the health of her whale populations. As long as humans continue to hunt whales, our kind continues to shed the blood of the *elemental* Earth. That is to say, the Godspark which empowered the creation of our world is bled away with the lifeblood of the whales, our oceanic ancestors.

For those who partake of whale medicine, be prepared with the aid of these Power Animals to embark on vast journeys no person could undergo alone. Family is important to whales who travel in pods and bring with them on their epic journeys all whom they love and with whom they share the deepest bonds. Whales carry much ancient knowledge, and those who are drawn to whale medicine will often discover they have a scholarly bent to study history, mythology, archaeology, anthropology, ecology, oceanography, and other similar topics.

Whale medicine is also about balance. The largest creatures on Earth, they are helpless on the shore but are fleet and graceful in the deep waters. They are also mammals and so are creatures of two worlds, air and water, masculine and feminine. Their organs collapse when they flounder or are driven out of their element, and this is a caution to us to be aware of our surroundings and our circumstances and take care to place ourselves in the healthiest and most nurturing environments or risk sometimes dire consequences.

Equines

Horse: I have a distant childhood memory of looking at my father's colored dinosaur books and wondering at the incredible creature called eohippus which eventually became the horse of today. Another more recent memory is of walking through rural Iowa and coming across a pasture where a horse and a mule stood silently together in solidarity and grief as the body of their deceased mule companion lay not far from them, bloating in the sun and forgotten by the humans. Indeed, the noble equines have endured across millennia, global climate changes, and the encroachment of humans into their lives.

Horses, above almost any other creature living in close contact with humans, have retained their wild hearts, even in the face of being "broken" emotionally in order to serve people for labor and transportation. Their spirits, I believe, are still intact nonetheless, as they have retained the ability to love one another, other animals, and human beings.

These are social creatures of the herd and require companionship and camaraderie to remain healthy, and the same is true of those people who are drawn to horse medicine or who have attracted horses as Power Animals. Horses have very keen senses and maintain a studied awareness of their environment, cautioning us to do the same. Particularly sensitive to energy and Spirit, horses scan their surroundings and assess the energetic currents at play as well as the underlying integrity of those with whom they come in contact.

Discerning, faithful, strong, loving, social, and in their essence still wild, the "unbridled" medicine of horses is powerful. These noble creatures, so often led to their doom, harshly treated, or neglected over the centuries by humans, cause us to look more deeply for the connections that bind us and to seek the forgiveness of the Animal Kingdom.

Felines

<u>Domestic Cats</u>: Cat says, "Love me for my graceful splendor." These regal, wild-hearted beings are true free spirits, and they will not be reshaped by humans or any other species. Strong and independent, cats provide an example of living life boldly on your own terms. Cats are loving and affectionate but will not be pressured into expressing their feelings. They demand respect, their own space, and their own good time but will quickly join a family member who is ill or unhappy in order to provide watchful care and companionship.

Hunters by nature, cats are extremely astute to all the goings-on around them and teach watchfulness. They are also patient hunters, waiting still and silent for just the right moment to pounce on the object of their attention. Cats are extremely spiritual animals, very sensitive to energy and spiritual presences and highly telepathic. Attuned to the people in her home, a cat will often reflect the health and vitality of the humans.

Human depression, anxiety, grief, and worry take a toll on cats (as well as all other household animal companions), and they will find creative ways of showing their dis-ease and displeasure such as inappropriate scratching, a sudden change in temperament, or not using the litter box. They sometimes will manifest physical illnesses as well. If the family cat is unhappy or unwell, it is usually a good time to explore the human dynamics that may be influencing their health and behavior. Animals who love us frequently take on the mantle of whatever plagues us, and they need to be gently reminded that this is not necessary. They also want and need to see us caring for our own needs.

<u>Tiger</u>: All cats teach gracefulness in some aspect of life. Tigers in particular focus on emotional grace. As a fearsome predator, the tiger has learned to use his powerful passions to maximum effect. He teaches us that, when challenged or injured by others, we need to be cautious lest our rage consume us like the wild,

unschooled beast that it can be. The tiger is not controlled by rage – he walks his anger on a leash, deriving strength from having been riled, using his temper as a tool, like a Samurai with his razor-sharp sword.

The tiger is wily and watchful at all times. Soft-footed and alert, he stalks his prey, knowing when to lie in wait and when to spring. He does not allow hunger or indignation to push him into an untimely indiscretion. He is fearless, his controlled emotions acting in harmony with his cleverness and physical agility, ensuring that he is most often the victor.

Forest Creatures

Rabbit: This creature asks that we be gentle. He advises us to live quickly, for life is short. An opportunity wasted may never come again. Speed must be balanced by spending quiet time in the burrow, taking stock of our lives and enjoying simple creature comforts.

Rabbits nurture a great gift of spiritual power held in their bosoms and passed on to the predator who consumes his physical form. Rabbits eat the tender living shoots warmed by the sun's rays. They travel beneath the moon's cold fire and feed on the silver-gilded leaves and blossoms that her light reveals. All who have kept a garden know that the Earth's choicest bounty is food for the rabbit – who then rests and incorporates his intake in the safety of his burrow, deep in the embrace of Mother Earth.

When the Great Horned Owl swoops upon his elusive prey,

he is grateful for the rabbit's life given to sustain his, and the earthy treasure of this creature, held like a bag of gems against his heart, is taken back to the raptor's nest. There, the bird will merge with the rabbit's harvested gems of sun and moon, nurtured in the Earth and borne to the sky by the owl – and the rabbit's gentle spirit springs away soundlessly in the forest, preparing for his rebirth.

Deer: The deer is a traveler, moving over the face of the Earth and becoming wise. He appreciates the spaciousness of life, and his hallmark is freedom. A deer may go anywhere, walking softly along trails, scrambling up hills and outcroppings of rock, to then run fleet and strong across meadows of green. He has no fear of being inappropriate, no concern for how others may see him. He knows the joys of the morning, the heavy slumber of afternoon, and the stars of night are his. His message to humans: Be gentle with yourself and offer kindness to all living things.

Insects

Butterfly: The butterfly has long been a Christian symbol for resurrection. Butterflies are beings of transformation, and they come into my life during times of creative change and emergence. As caterpillars, they are earthbound and vulnerable, creatures who seek the shelter of leaves and deep places. Spinning their silken cocoons, they create their own vehicles of change, self-made havens of retreat from which they come forth remade. They are never stuck at the beginning but progress smoothly through their process of evolution, encouraging us to act as they do on faith and natural wisdom in order to grow and to become.

Butterflies are bridgers, creatures of two worlds and of two births. Spirits of the air, they choose their times and places to alight on the Earth, grounding with Source and taking nourishment while dazzling with their beauty and inspiring awe with their fluttering freedom. We too start life in the body as creatures of the Earth, born of her womb and seeking nurture as we climb the ladder of the chakras into the sky, emerging finally through the crown as the limitless, Source-connected beings of infinite potential that we were always meant to become. Delight in the presence of butterflies as harbingers of opportunity for growth and progression and as a living example of the inner buds of beauty in each of us, seeking only time and nurture to blossom into perfect flower.

Reptiles

Turtles: The turtle is the embodiment of the caution, "Don't underestimate me!" Slow and graceless on land, the turtle is another creature of two worlds, swift and graceful in the water like the butterfly is fleet in the air. Their halting gait in the mud or sand is an incomplete picture of who and what the turtle really is. The hands and feet that anchor them in their slow tread upon the Earth are valuable paddles in the water, natural oars that steer them swiftly through the currents of life.

Turtles also teach the lesson that our "safe harbor" is not an object such as a house or barricade. Rather, it is a part of us, something we must carry with us everywhere on our journey through life. Turtles travel light and yet with everything they need on their backs.

When turtles come into your life, see this as a reminder to go with the flow in your own element in order to achieve grace and ease – and no matter how landlocked we may seem, we too have another nature, a spiritual nature that yearns to be carried by crystal streams. Also remember that safety and security are always within reach, within the knowing of the Higher Self.

Most people equate the imagination with unreality. Nothing could be further from the truth. The imagination is a power of the mind to create and work with images. It is this ability which can open us to other realms, assist us in healing, help us to discover lost knowledge and to open to higher vision and even prophecy. (p. 8, Andrews, 1993)

-- *Ted Andrews*

Telepathic Animal Communication

Although I have been a spirit medium since childhood and have worked on numerous paranormal investigations with Two Rivers Paranormal Society, my first experiences with telepathic animal communication occurred when I began practicing Reiki with animals, and I became convinced that the Reiki energy was creating a spiritual or soul-level bond between me and the animals, enabling a very easy and natural flow of information not subject to the impediments of language. Reiki treatments often involve receiving images, thoughts, and emotions from animals.

As I widened the circle of people and animals with whom I worked, I felt the challenges and chafed against the limitations of a culture that largely dismisses or downgrades telepathy and metaphysics, and I sought ways to honor my perceptions and validate my intuitive hits. I attended an animal communication workshop led by Karen Craft, a telepathic animal communicator and Shamanic Reiki Master who authored the book *The Cosmic*

Purr. She taught that telepathy is the universal language of interspecies communication and that our companion animals are speaking to us all the time. She states that we receive energetic vibrations and impulses from animals that we are able to process through our own filters and translate into our human languages.

The ancients also believed that telepathy was a universal language across species. In India, it was believed that animals communicated in their own mysterious tongues for which the gods had a natural faculty and could therefore communicate with animals directly. Human beings, however, need to practice the psychic ability of telepathy and work to become conscious of what we glean from the energy fields of other beings.

Karen Craft observes that we put words into the mouths of our animals all the time: "He's scared of the fireworks." "She's jealous of her brother." "He's feeling all cooped up." She believes that much of this is based on real intuitive understanding and that everyone has the ability to be an animal communicator, with or without the use of Reiki or other modalities. For her, animal communication is about being in a heart-centered place and being in the present moment. Indeed, any practice that links us with an animal's energy field – such as mindfulness, Reiki, or meditation – creates an effortless way for animals to share in their native language of telepathy.

One of the most important communication skills we can develop is listening, which is more than just hearing but is also *observing* and taking note at the physical and energetic levels. It requires a high level of attentiveness and involvement with another being to recognize and comprehend all the messages being sent to us. Animals are experts at this. They study us in detail, learning to comprehend subtle shadings of emotion in our vocal tones, facial expressions, and body language. They are also very receptive to the energetic shifts in our auras that accompany varying emotions, physical reactions, and states of health.

Animals want our attention as they frequently communicate

with us in subtle ways that we disregard or fail to recognize. We must start by learning the body language of animals and learning to interpret the meaning of their voices. For example, a dog in a bowing posture wants to play, and a dog in a crouching posture or slowly creeping forward is stalking and preparing to spring, either in fun or in earnest. Subtle growls generally mean, "Leave me alone – I want my space." More guttural emissions are a sterner warning to beware. There's the loud, single bark that puts the pack on alert, and the joyous whines and howls of a dog greeting his favorite person in the world at the end of a long day apart.

When you have learned to understand the physical, you can move to understanding the metaphysical messages that animals are sending. This is a challenge in a society where intuition is devalued and we have lost many of our connections to the natural world. Just try going with your instinctive understandings, and instead of worrying that you are "wrong" or "making it up," see where they lead you and give yourself a chance to be "right." The more you acknowledge and honor intuitive hits, the easier it becomes to tap the deep well of interspecies understanding.

One of my early animal communication experiences was for a woman whose dog was being housed a thousand miles away with a relative while the woman was traveling due to changed life circumstances. She was in tears at the separation and wanted to make sure her dog understood that she loved her and was coming back for her. She also wanted desperately to find a way to continue their close bond across the miles.

Using Reiki to create a bridge and looking at a photograph, I was able to connect with the dog immediately. She was able to describe her new yard in detail down to the bare red earth and lack of grass, the climate, and her favorite activities. She also expressed great concern for her person, which the woman had known would be her dog's top priority, and wanted to ensure that the woman had adequate support from friends throughout her travels.

I was able to reassure both the dog and the woman that the other was doing okay, and I could state with certainty that the dog was happy in her new surroundings, missed and loved her mom, and understood that the situation was temporary. This woman was shocked at how accurately I could describe a back-yard and a property in Texas – but really I was just relaying images and messages from the dog.

Similarly, a distance animal Reiki client was stunned, asking how I could possibly know that her cats had been temporarily displaced from their bedroom sanctum. Well, I hadn't known at all – but the cats certainly did, and they were very eager to express their frustration and desire to move back in. They had previously tried to communicate this through inappropriate behaviors, but with the vehicle of Reiki were able to state the reason behind their naughtiness.

These experiences cemented for me that all Lightworkers and mediums have to work in their own ways. Reiki is my way, and it's the foundation piece for all of my work with both animals and people. Many people successfully communicate with animals without ever learning Reiki. Some mediums rely on channeled information from Guides, opening the Akashic Records, and other methods. There is no right or wrong way to communicate. What matters is that the communication comes through.

Buddy Speaks From Beyond the Veil: An amazing telepath-ic experience which completely altered and expanded my views about the spiritual roles of animals occurred when my friend

Suzette Schmidt asked me to perform mediumship with her deceased Labrador Retriever, Buddy, to ask about his potential to reincarnate. The information which came through made me realize that I previously had only a small vision of what animals could do in the Realms we inhabit.

Buddy explained that he was presently doing very important work in the Spiritual Realm, and it appeared that he was retrieving and helping to catalog or archive knowledge in the Akashic Records. He had been assigned and was overseen in this work by an Angel of great stature wearing a black cowl and golden robes and wings, a staff or stave in his right hand. Buddy was very proud of this work and wanted to continue it; otherwise, he would be prepared to return to Suzette sooner rather than later.

Suzette and I reminded Buddy that, in the spiritual family in which he'd been raised, he knew how to meditate and even to astral travel, as he had done both frequently while alive. He indicated that, if he could be reassured that through astral travel he could continue his Spirit Realm work while reincarnated in a body, and be "outside of time" while travelling so that no "time was lost" from this higher-purpose work, he would be happy to return. He wished to be reminded of and reinforced in these abilities, and Archangel Gabriel came forward to offer personal assistance with this process.

Suzette Schmidt is an intuitive medium who opens and interprets the Akashic Records and also works in a university library. Buddy explained he is not only going to work with his person in spirit each day, he is also going to his own work in a Records Library, and that his training during his lifetime with his person prepared him for his higher purpose. It also came through that Buddy would, in fact, be collaborating with Suzette in her own Akashic Records work once he reincarnated, and that the last lifetime was a building block to the next.

Suzette wanted to know if Buddy would remember that he

was Buddy, who she was, and the life they had shared. Buddy explained that animals have "cosmic memory," and that they carry memories of past lives with them through the veil and into the next incarnation. This is something that most humans are not able to do, and Buddy suggested that humans need to learn this from animals, as our soul growth and spiritual development would be heightened by the retention of pertinent memories from across the continuum.

At the end of the mediumship session, he indicated only "puppy" regarding his return and could not or would not state any further details. I was shown an image on the left of a chalice shaped like a single cupped hand. This was a symbol for the place of Buddy's rebirth. On the right appeared an alligator who opened her huge jaws to release a single large egg which then traveled to the chalice. The alligator was to be a sign for how Suzette would know Buddy upon his reincarnation. I was confused about the egg emerging from the mouth of the alligator; I had thought of alligators as eaters of the eggs of other animals.

A study of alligator medicine revealed that alligators "are known as the keepers of ancient wisdom" and connected to the acquisition and guardianship of primal knowledge. This certainly fit with Buddy's new role with the Akashic Records. We also learned that the mother alligator is one of the best mothers in the Animal Kingdom. She takes into her mouth any of her eggs from which the baby is having difficulty emerging, gently breaking the shell with her teeth to assist with the birthing process. (Woolcott, "Alligator/Crocodile Power Animal," n.d.)

It became clear then that the sign was this: Buddy will incarnate in a puppy who is the product of a difficult birth, possibly a puppy who has difficulty emerging from the amniotic sac. Alligator was also serving as additional reinforcement for Buddy's new vocation with spiritual records.

The information that came through from Buddy in this session was nothing short of awe-inspiring. That night, as I looked at my dog Reggie sleeping peacefully with his head on my husband's shoulder, I realized that we really had very little idea of who and what animals really are, even those closest to us. The energies of this New Age are not only for people. This is also a time to break down barriers between humans and animals and dismantle the internal structures that keep us from true understanding and appreciation of the amazing creatures with whom we share Physical Reality.

Deeper Communication With Your Animals

A Guided Visualization Exercise

- When an animal is displaying troubling behavior, and you're at your wits' end trying to modify or correct it...
- When your furry or feathered companion has a physical or emotional symptom that has the veterinarian at a loss...
- When an animal family member is having difficulty coping with a new environment or other lifestyle change...

Meditation can help you tune out distractions and tune in to your animal's energy, meeting him on a level where no barriers to communication exist. The following is a technique I've developed that can be used by anyone. You can be physically present with your animal, touching or holding your animal, or merely holding him in thought across any distance. If you've received a Reiki attunement and have been given the distance healing symbol, you can use this to strengthen a long-distance connection. Remember, animals are natural telepaths and already know how to talk to us. Humans are the ones that need practice with this.

Sit comfortably in a quiet space where you'll be free from interruption. Turn off the TV, telephones, and other distractions.

Take several deep breaths. See the breath as an energetic mist. It might be white or pink or golden, or it might have no color at all. The in-breath moves from your lungs into your limbs and throughout your body, filling you with strength and peace. The out-breath releases the clutter of your thoughts, your worries from the day, gentling dislodging them and sending them out into the atmosphere. Concentrate on the in and out flows of this breath, gently untangling and smoothing out, energizing and cleansing, a soft tide moving over the sand and then flowing out beyond the horizon.

In this space of calm, visualize your chakras, the energy centers of your being, like seven flowers of light, multicolored stars or wheels in all colors of the rainbow. You want them to be open like petals in the sun and spin with a steady rotation. This gives you strength and balance.

The root chakra is a deep red lotus of light, placed like a tail that reaches down into Mother Earth, grounding you, a passageway into the primal intelligence we share with all living things.

At the base of your spine is the sacral chakra. Feel its warm energy spirals in a brilliant orange, the color of embers and ripe fruit.

The solar plexus chakra shines through your midsection with a golden light and the warmth of the sun. Its element is fire and it is the seat of your personal power.

The lotus of luminous green is the heart chakra. Its light is the color of new life, a green blossom with a rose quartz center, and it bathes your heart, the place where you step between the worlds. It is where you know and hear all the company of Nature.

Your throat chakra is a brilliant blue, and it energizes your thoughts and your imagination. See it spinning like a blue galaxy in a dark sky or like a star engulfed in the blue waters of the sea. Feel its spin, its cooling colors of cobalt and sapphire shining like a beacon, illuminating ideas.

The brow chakra is your third eye in the center of your forehead, indigo and amethyst, the glowing of the midnight sky between the worlds. This is a chakra of the senses, of second sight, and windows into hidden worlds and unknown treasure. See with this eye now, expanding your vision far beyond the physical world, seeing across all spaces and all times.

The crown chakra is the thousand-petalled lotus, a beacon of violet white and silver white at the very top of the head. Here stretches a clear crystal bridge into infinity, astral travel, and Unity with the Divine. See the Divine Spirit in all things, from a blade of grass, to a stone, to a mountain goat and the mountain he crosses. Bathe in these colors of purest white and brightest reality.

Your chakras are open wide and their rainbow lights surround you in the shape of your body, sometimes shimmering, sometimes steady, sometimes bold or subtle. As you experience this energetic body, reach out with your arms of light to your beloved animal. See him surrounded by his own light body, his own glimmering rainbow of chakra colors, and beckon him to come close, into your field, into your heart of light. Ask him, in the wordless language of spirit, if he will join you in a space of love and openness. Call to him by name, and let him come to you.

If he agrees to unite with you, take a moment to experience his presence and the merging of your energy fields. Do you sense the pureness of heart of your animal? Do you feel the trueness and sincerity with which animals speak? For you are speaking even now, you and your animal, without speech or gestures or anything complicated, but in the most elemental way. Thank him and praise him for joining you, and know it for the privilege that it is.

You may now show him images of what concerns you and share your inmost thoughts. Tell him how you are feeling and what it is you wish to know. This is the time to ask: Why? What is wrong? How do you feel? What do you want or need? How can I help? Express your love and support. Reassure your animal that it is all right for him to tell you anything he wishes to.

And now you must listen with your heart. Create a cocoon of love and light and use all your higher senses – your intuition, inner knowing, the vision of the mind's eye where mysteries are revealed. You may see images from your animal's past or present. You may feel in your own body an ache or pain he is sharing from his body. You may have a flash of insight about your animal that wasn't there before. Trust your instincts and your emotions as animals do.

Continue to share in this way until you sense it is time to come back. Thank him and honor what he has shared. Then gently separate your energies, concentrating again on the breath. Move apart with the in-breath, and with the out-breath settle more solidly back into your physical body until you are fully present, returned with a deepened bond with your animal and a greater understanding.

If you have made promises, it is important to keep them lest you lose your animal's trust. Keep faith with him, and take positive action on what you have learned.

It is important to always remember that we never 'own' an animal, we are their companions, their care-givers, their healers. We can never own another soul, whether it be human or animal. (p. 82, Coates, 2003)

— Margrit Coates

The Concern for Animal Souls

Let there be no equivocation on this point: *Animals have souls.* The spiritual essence of an animal is as eternal and enduring as that of a human being. The deep empathic love, loyalty, and devotion that humans share with animals is a bond which can only be achieved at the deepest soul-to-soul level. We are responsible for right action toward and feeling for the animal beings with whom we share the earth.

The noble creatures of air and water and land are eternal beings of a high and mystical order, a truth well-known to the ancients. To Hippocrates (physician and philosopher, 460-377 BC) is attributed the statement, "The soul is the same for all living creatures, although the body of each is different." Pythagoras (mathematician and philosopher, 570-495 BC) declared, "Animals share with us the privilege of having a soul."

There is sometimes hairsplitting in the use of the words *soul* and *spirit.* A Gnostic understanding is that the soul is the temporary housing for the incarnated spirit which is the true spark of God. In such a context, I believe that animals, like humans, have both soul *and* spirit. Throughout this book, however, I use the words soul and spirit interchangeably as does the popular culture, and in every case, I intend to state that animals possess Divine Godspark which returns to Unity with Source.

Anyone who has witnessed the unbridled joy of a dog chasing a ball or scenting through a field knows that this dog is invested absolutely in the living moment of his experience. When I rejoin my animal children after the absence of a day or only an hour, their full and enthusiastic focus is on the exchanging of love, and their wholehearted greeting is given unstintingly without the distractions of watching a clock, worrying about tomorrow, or reliving some prior angst.

Clearly, animals already know the secret of free and joyous living – how to be fully in the present moment, the only real moment that exists – with which humans must struggle mightily. This may be taken as a modern example of the ancient spiritual belief that animals, amongst the rest of the creation, remained closer than humans to the Divine and that these more energetically attuned creatures model many spiritual truths humanity has yet to embrace. A Gnostically inspired view is that, as spirits living in an inherently flawed creation, animals, in their descent to this realm, have retained more of the innate spiritual wisdom from Source to which humans are often blinded by the chatter of the mind and the distractions of the created Universe.

I am an Ordained Minister of Wisdom of the Heart Church, a church of metaphysics, and I identify myself as a Christian mystic, esoteric/Gnostic Christian, or Christian metaphysician. In my spiritual ministry, my primary focus is on animals and those who love and care for them. A deep well of need exists among these populations – a need for prayer, healing, assistance with end-of-life-transition, and grief support. I also see a need for a spiritual leader to conduct burial and memorial services for animals, bless an animal adoption, or simply say a few words or lead a prayer to consecrate a memorial stone or other keepsake.

I believe in the concept that animals do not reside as far

from the presence and knowledge of the Divine as humanity presently does. This being the case, animals and indeed the totality of the Nature Kingdom are humankind's bridges back to Divinity. It is through connections with animals and the natural world – which animals comprehend with such superior depth and breadth of understanding and experience – that we will ascend Jacob's ladder and return to the Unity of Being which we have either forgotten or discarded.

Great spiritual teachers like Edgar Cayce and Buddha have suggested that Unity with other soul beings in the Christ Consciousness or Universal Intelligence or The Collective – together as one and as companions of God – is the highest goal for humans. The souls of animals also unite with the Christ Consciousness, and to me this indicates equal access to the Divine among the souls of different species – and perhaps total equality – an idea in radical contrast to the strict linear hierarchy of modern Western culture with humans at the top and animals lumped together at the bottom.

At a spiritual gathering for 2012 that included rock divination and Nature augery, I asked, "What I should tell the world about animal spirituality?" Three themes predominated.

- I was told to remind people to be awed at the sheer variety of animal species and their specialized adaptations, from a chameleon changing color to a mountain goat gripping a cliff. We may see some animals like seahorses or kangaroos as strange, misfit creatures. In reality, these are perfectly adapted beings, and we must view them in their own context and according to their unique realities.

- We need to begin comprehending through the use of other, lost senses and learn to emulate the native wisdom of animals. Animals are teachers, imparters of wisdom, and ones who see with a deeper and more penetrating vision.

- Humanity threw away much which was very precious when we decided to become "civilized," casting off treasures torn loose by disconnecting from Nature. We have, to a degree, lost our ability to love. There is something missing from human nature that animals can return to us. It can be found by reconnecting to the natural world.

A woman recently discussed with me her lingering feelings of guilt and doubt at having made the decision to euthanize a very elderly and beloved dog whose limbs had failed to the extent that he could no longer avoid falling into his feces when he relieved himself. She said that she wanted him to "be allowed to die with dignity." Momentarily forgetting our culture's distinctions, she said, "But we took a human life," having decided on the administration of an injection "that stopped his heart."

But we took a human life. Those simple words speak volumes about the love this woman felt toward her dog and show clearly that her actions were founded in that love. To me, this is what is most important. She made her decision from the right place – her heart – and she had a clear sense of her dog companion's place in the world and of the sacred interconnectedness of life.

Regarding questions about euthanasia, I advise clients that animals see life and death differently than we do, more attuned as they are to the turning of the wheel and of Self as an eternal being of Spirit. First, however, I would counsel an animal's human to look into his or her heart and examine the feelings that reside there. Both animals and people occasionally err in judgment, but I believe that in this case, a loving intention and caring commitment is what matters most. If we ultimately decide that we made a mistake either for or against euthanasia, the animals with whom we share the bond of unconditional love will forgive us as we must also forgive ourselves.

All that can be asked of anyone is to make the most loving and compassionate decision for an animal. I do not believe that there is always only one correct answer to the question of how to face an animal's final infirmity or illness. One may need to wrestle with his or her views regarding euthanasia of humans if one truly sees no difference in the quality of an animal's soul.

If an animal is terminally ill and no longer able to enjoy a sufficient quality of life to make continuation in the body worthwhile, I personally believe that the decision to euthanize is a valid one. I do not believe that there is any virtue to be gained from suffering for the sake of suffering, and if pointless physical anguish can be alleviated, I think it ought to be. However, I would strongly advise getting more than one veterinary opinion if there is any doubt about the animal's diagnosis or prognosis or the qualifications of the physician. I would suggest asking about palliative measures such as pain medications, acupuncture, or energy work that may improve an aged or ill animal's quality of life.

It is also worthwhile to contact an animal communicator or animal intuitive to speak psychically with the animal and learn what his or her personal wishes are, answer any questions the animal may have, and assist with final messages and goodbyes if the animal desires. Animals are very wise about choosing a course of action at these times and should be consulted. They may also need assistance to transition off the physical plane, just as human beings sometimes do. Animals will always talk to the humans they love, but sometimes it is very difficult for the people involved to be open to those messages, particularly when the emotions are highly charged, such as around the issues of injury, illness, and death.

I also must emphasize the unqualified need for *humane* euthanasia if this option is chosen. With inadequate legislation to protect animals in Western society, we each personally owe it to our animals to make certain that their lives are ended peacefully by an injection from a qualified veterinary professional if it has been decided to euthanize. I believe that animals should be prepared for the end of life using Reiki, healing touch, animal communication, prayer, calling upon the Angels, and/or other compassionate techniques. I also feel that a loved one should be with the animal when he or she dies if at all possible. If the animal's humans are not able to deal with this or cannot be present, an animal Reiki practitioner, spiritual counselor, healer, or a caring worker from the veterinary clinic may be asked to be present.

Our final acts at the close of an animal's physical life should pay tribute to the love and devotion we shared during that life. Then our focus must switch to the things that are eternal.

Only the physical bodies of our beloved animal companions die, as do our own. The flesh is temporary, but the soul remains forever, not bound by the strictures of life span that govern biological organisms. We *will* be together again.

As a Minister and a metaphysician, a psychic medium and Reiki Master, I have been privileged to assist with a number of animal life-to-Light transitions. Whether I'm at a veterinary clinic or a in a private home, when I'm called to help with an animal who is dying I have never failed to be awed and humbled at the courage and acceptance with which animals face physical death. Perhaps it is their greater capacity to access information from past lives that affords them faith in rebirth. Animals live closer to Spirit and Divine things than humans, and this too helps them on their way.

As I've said, sometimes animals need help with their transition process. Many animals are "old souls" who have incarnated before and become acquainted with a variety of spirit beings, both light and dark. In one emergency session for a dying cat, I became aware of a spirit in human shape repeatedly peeking from behind a wall and then retreating. I asked his identity, and he indicated that he had been a pharaoh or some soul being from Egypt that the cat had known before; I was not convinced.

It felt like a trickster spirit showing up at this animal's time of death, and I asked for him to be banished and for Jesus Christ to come in immediately. Jesus quickly and completely abolished this uncomfortable presence, and indeed, the entire Holy Family was guarding this cat. Archangel Michael and Guardian Angels made themselves visible, and I brought in a trusted disincarnate cat spirit to lead the way as well. While I was distressed by this faceless spirit, it was a relief to know that the highest level Divine help will rush to an animal's aid and protection. We have only to ask for this, and it will be done.

Consistently, I have seen animals make the journey through death surrounded by Angelic helpers, Ascended Masters, Spirit Guides, the souls of pre-deceased loves ones, and other beings of compassion. Their souls do not depart the Earth alone but in the company of Light and love. I have witnessed their portals and passages to the Spiritual Realm in many forms, images sent by the animals and their Guardians that enable me to comprehend that soul's crossing and communicate about it with the bereaved. The beauty and wonder of the sacred journeys of animals into Spirit must be made known again to the world at large.

Soul Transition Case Study: Mittens the Cat

Mittens was a lovely elderly cat at Animal Lifeline. I received an email that Mittens had been ill and, despite the staff's best efforts, she had been losing weight and had finally stopped eating. The painful decision was made that the kindest action was to humanely euthanize her. "She was 15 years old and tired," the email read. "While in my arms she made the journey to the other side." The director asked me if I would contact Mittens and make sure she was okay.

Sadly, Mittens was the first of two animals who passed away in rapid succession at the shelter, so I prepared a session for both of them. I generally call in specific Divine beings for the transitioning process. In this case, I sought assistance from Jesus; Archangels Michael (protector), Raphael (safe travel, restoring lost animals, healing), Ariel (Nature and Animal Kingdom), and Gabriel (communication); my personal Power Animals; and the specific Guardian Spirits of the animals who had passed away. I also set up a crystal layout for energetic support.

Mittens presented to me readily, and strengthening and healing were given at all levels including the soul level. Mittens wished to say goodbye to Amie the Cat and showed a clear image of Amie. She also shared an image of a woman's left hand gently touching the front of her body. She was grateful for the compassion and love she received at the shelter. She was peaceful. She was ready to depart at the time she did.

I saw a clear image of her Guardian Angels soaring upward while shepherding a bright light (Mittens's soul). However, Mittens remained behind for a few minutes as she provided an image of her body and communicated her final messages. I then saw the transfiguration of Mittens from a physical body to a soul body, and she appeared as a beautiful sphere of light with a heart of amethyst purple and layer upon layer of lighter colors radiating outward. Her Angels ascended upward with this beautiful sphere of light and then set it free to continue its upward flight into the realm of Spirit, and I was privileged to watch this until the light disappeared from sight into the distant sky.

After sending a written report to the shelter, the director thanked me for the session, adding that this work was helpful to the staff in coping with the loss of the animals. She added, "I think the lady's hand Mittens was referring to was mine. I was stroking her with my left hand and talking to her during the process."

Soul Transition Case Study: Pepper the Dog

Pepper was a lively, seven-month-old German Shepherd mix puppy who arrived at Animal Lifeline after being placed on death row in a shelter with a high kill rate. He had received no medical care during his six weeks at the previous shelter and was suffering from a severe urinary tract infection, Giardia, round worms, and a broken right front leg that had never been set and resulted in deformity.

At Animal Lifeline, Pepper was finally receiving the antibiotics and deworming medication he had so desperately needed, and an orthopaedic specialist was consulted about the broken limb. The doctors felt they could save the leg and avoid amputation, and surgery was undertaken. Tragically, Pepper went into cardiac arrest near the end of his procedure, and despite their best efforts, the veterinary team couldn't save him. His death was a shocking blow, ending our hopes for his forever home.

The night Pepper passed away, I pledged to contact him, explain what had happened, and make sure he crossed over appropriately. Sending out the Reiki energy, I called to the puppy's soul, seeking a connection.

I found that, not knowing what to do in the wake of his sudden death, Pepper had returned to the shelter. He did not seem afraid, just somewhat muddled and foggy-headed. He was resting on his stomach (on his knees and elbows) and appeared to be licking or chewing a bone or toy. With the abruptness of his passing, he did not understand what had happened.

Strength and healing were given at all levels. I explained that he had undergone surgery on his leg, his body had died, and he could not return to it. I told him that only his body was gone, and his soul was bright and vibrant. I explained that it was time to go to Rainbow Bridge and await the call of the person whose heart is linked with his or else go on to the higher realms of Spirit. It was time for new adventures and no more suffering with worms, infection, or an injured leg. In short, it was time to leave the shelter.

Pepper wished to be held and comforted first, and we sat like this for a while as I stroked his energy body. He indicated that the shelter is "nice." I then became aware of him beginning to materialize on a different plane of existence where dawn seemed to be breaking, and I believe that this is Rainbow Bridge.

I saw a large and beautiful flame of many colors. I saw this flame burn for several minutes, and then it began an ascent through the darkness, many hands reaching upward towards it as it departed; this was the soul of Pepper being sent on his journey by a host of Angelic beings. This flame ascended into the sky like an arrowhead – an arrow in flight – until at last it passed from my view.

Animals and the Afterlife

Allowing that animals are complex energy beings who possess soul bodies, where do these souls go when their physical bodies have perished? I have found evidence of a wide array of choices for these animal souls. Hinduism and Buddhism both espouse a belief in animal reincarnation, either as another animal or as a human being.

Abstract religious thought forms are useful as guides and as the foci of deeper questioning. However, I wanted to uncover the sort of knowledge that can only come from deeply personal interaction with animals – the glimpses of the afterlife that have been offered by the animals themselves.

We had a very profound experience with The Rainbow Bridge. My husband Benjamin entered a shamanic journey state and was met by a dog Spirit Guide named Jack who took him to what he later described as Doggie Heaven. Ben told me about a green, park-like expanse of trees and meadows where dogs of all kinds played or rested in the sun. Occasionally, a dog would turn and listen, only to run off joyfully. Jack explained that the dogs in this place were waiting. When their people joined them on the Other Side, they would call their dogs to them in a loving reunion. My husband was very affected by this vision and recounted the story several times to our friends.

At an animal shelter many months later, he saw a framed copy of *The Rainbow Bridge* hanging on a wall beside shelves of urns that held the cremations of beloved dogs and cats. He turned to me in complete shock. This poem was an exact recounting of his meditative journey. Neither one of us had ever seen or heard it before. Skeptics might claim this to be a very precise and detailed coincidence. As far as Ben is concerned, Rainbow Bridge is a very real place in the Spiritual Realm which he has visited and experienced for himself, together with a guiding canine spirit.

THE RAINBOW BRIDGE POEM

WHEN AN ANIMAL DIES THAT HAS BEEN ESPECIALLY CLOSE TO SOMEONE HERE, THAT PET GOES TO RAINBOW BRIDGE. THERE ARE MEADOWS AND HILLS FOR ALL OF OUR SPECIAL FRIENDS SO THEY CAN RUN AND PLAY TOGETHER. THERE IS PLENTY OF FOOD, WATER, AND SUNSHINE, AND OUR FRIENDS ARE WARM AND COMFORTABLE.

ALL THE ANIMALS WHO HAD BEEN ILL AND OLD ARE RESTORED TO HEALTH AND VIGOR. THOSE WHO WERE HURT OR MAIMED ARE MADE WHOLE AND STRONG AGAIN, JUST AS WE REMEMEBER THEM IN OUR DREAMS OF DAYS AND TIMES GONE BY. THE ANIMALS ARE HAPPY AND CONTENT, EXCEPT FOR ONE SMALL THING; THEY EACH MISS SOMEONE VERY SPECIAL TO THEM, WHO HAD TO BE LEFT BEHIND.

THEY ALL RUN AND PLAY TOGETHER, BUT THE DAY COMES WHEN ONE SUDDENLY STOPS AND LOOKS INTO THE DISTANCE. HIS BRIGHT EYES ARE INTENT. HIS EAGER BODY QUIVERS. SUDDENLY HE BEGINS TO RUN FROM THE GROUP, FLYING OVER THE GREEN GRASS, HIS LEGS CARRYING HIM FASTER AND FASTER.

YOU HAVE BEEN SPOTTED, AND WHEN YOU AND YOUR SPECIAL FRIEND FINALLY MEET, YOU CLING TOGETHER IN JOYOUS REUNION, NEVER TO BE PARTED AGAIN. THE HAPPY KISSES RAIN UPON YOUR FACE; YOUR HANDS AGAIN CARESS THE BELOVED HEAD, AND YOU LOOK ONCE MORE INTO THE TRUSTING EYES OF YOUR PET, SO LONG GONE FROM YOUR LIFE BUT NEVER ABSENT FROM YOUR HEART.

THEN YOU CROSS RAINBOW BRIDGE TOGETHER...

– AUTHOR UNKNOWN

In my Reiki practice, I've encountered a lot of amazing animals, but one of the wisest in the ways of the soul was a cat called Cosmo, an eighteen-year-old Himalayan with whom I was privileged to work several times in the final months of his life. I had been asked to do Reiki for his overall health and wellbeing and to make him as comfortable as possible in his senior years.

One day at our regular monthly session, Cosmo told me that he had started contemplating his transition and what he would do in the world of Spirit. He indicated that he was a very old soul who had traveled in and out of many incarnations, briefly indicating a lifetime in ancient Egypt. He also told me that he wanted to remain with his human mother for a time as a Spirit Guide before reincarnating again. He said that she would not have to make any terrible decision for him about euthanasia; he was going to make his own decision and go on his own terms when the time was right.

I knew that this was something I had to convey to Cosmo's person, and I tread carefully, since his impending transition was not apparent at that time. I told her gently that Cosmo "was thinking about the future" and explained that he was thinking a lot about his next phase in the Spiritual Realm. We scheduled a distance Reiki session for two weeks.

By the time of that session, Cosmo had largely stopped eating and had begun to sleep all the time, barely changing position. It appeared that his transition was steadily approaching. It seemed as though he had needed me to prepare his human, and once this was done, he had felt able to begin letting go.

During our session, Cosmo showed me a celestial pool, like a reflecting pond of water, where he had gone to drink. In many ancient religions and traditions, pools of water are portals to other dimensions of reality; I believe that this pool is such a place, and one with which Cosmo was familiar and to which he had returned. Looking down into the pool, I saw the upside-down reflection of a lovely being appearing as a young woman with alabaster skin wearing a headdress of great green leaves like cabbage leaves.

I attempted to look up and see who was standing at the pool, but I saw only blackness. I asked this being if she was a Spirit Guide or an Angel, and she replied, "I am The Guardian of Souls." Not *a* guardian of souls, or the guardian of a *particular* soul, but *The Guardian*.

Who was this being, and how could I know if she was benevolent? I asked for information from the Archangels, Jesus, Mother Mary, and my trusted Guides. This Guardian of Souls became rather vexed with me and seemed unused to being put through a vetting process! Indeed, she told me that she was much older than the incarnation of Jesus who was a mere 2000 years of age in that identity. I learned that The Guardian of Souls is a primeval being, a spirit of vast age akin to an Elemental or perhaps a nature spirit dating from the time of the creation. Mother Mary appeared in the vicinity of the pool wearing a blue mantle, indicating her approval of this being and her connection to the Divine Feminine.

Finally, another appeared to me in this pool to which Cosmo had gone. Looking like a charcoal sketch on white paper was the one I call The Tree Being, a figure in a rough robe with a great branching tree instead of a head and shoulders, numerous faces like The Green Man appearing in the boughs.

I did extensive work with Reiki Master and Lightworker Victoria Swanson to discover more about the identity of these mysterious beings. Whereas Mother Mary is the Divine Mother of all humankind, The Guardian of Souls seems to have a similar role in the Animal Kingdom. It was also suggested that she was perhaps actually *inside* the pool – i.e. in another dimension – as opposed to being a reflection upon its surface, which is why I saw nothing when I looked ahead at the spot where I expected her to be standing.

The Tree Being gives no name, but showed Victoria an impression of a tree standing still in the forest. The moment one looks away, the tree "runs" to another spot, and the startled human whirls around only to be uncertain of what he sees. The tree then takes another opportunity to rearrange itself within the person's peripheral vision and again confounds him. This being prefers to remain an enigma, showing himself only as a sketch and refusing to disclose an identity. He has a masculine energy that seems to balance the feminine of The Guardian of Souls, like a yin-yang harmony in the Spiritual Realm. He indicated that his function is to make me look twice or even three or four times, and to teach me that things are not as they seem to be.

When I first described this being to Victoria, she became very excited, telling me of The Findhorn Tree, a spirit seen at the mystical Findhorn garden by one of its founders. I had never seen or heard of this spirit before, but Victoria felt that my description was uncannily like a drawing she had seen. (I eventually located a drawing called "Oak Deva" by Brian Nobbs of Findhorn).

Hours before Cosmo made his transition, we had one last hands-on Reiki session with a lepidolite wand to assist his soul with the process of detaching and journeying. "I'm on the Path of Light," he said, "The Path of the Sun." He showed me a clear image of deep red rock canyons, a red earthen path between them leading to a glowing, golden-white orb of light. Cosmo was on this path, shaking out his abundant fur, the sunlight of the orb painting highlights on his body. He ran playfully along the path away from the sun, and then turned back. He was taking his own time and would choose his moment carefully. He was too regal a being to be rushed.

I thanked him for all he had taught me in our work together, and he asked, "Is there anything else I can teach you?" "Yes," I said. "What can I say to comfort your mother?" His answer was this: "Tell her that she knows my true Nature, she knows my true Essence and that we can never be separated." Indeed, since his passing, Cosmo has made himself known many times physically and psychically and remains a powerful presence. We should be awestruck at the lifetimes of wisdom imparted so effortlessly by a cat.

Afterlife Case Study: Wally, Watchdog Spirit

Wally was a special dog, even at a shelter that caters exclusively to special-needs animals. A Mastiff/American Bulldog mix who arrived at Animal Lifeline of Iowa in a pitiful state, he was a sweet giant, brave and steadfast with a boundless heart. When he became sick and racked with pain, after a life of neglect, his person committed a final heinous act of betrayal, chaining Wally to a stinking portable toilet in the woods and leaving him to die.

Gentle Wally lived seven months at the shelter, where the devoted staff had made it their mission that he would know unconditional love before he left this Earth. Showing love and grace and gratitude for these humans despite the cruelty he had endured at the hands of another, Wally began a mission of his own that continued after his physical death.

Wrapped up in Wally's story as it unfolded on the Internet in shelter photos and updates, I felt this sweet dog gently and persistently grab at my heart. His coat was a patchy mess, his skin was crusted and sore, his feet were infected and swollen with malignant tumors, he had hip dysplasia – and he stood in his footbath like a trooper, relished his rides to the vet in the shelter van, took delight in his plush new bed, and loved the bighearted people who reached out to him. When his pictures were suddenly taken down, I had hoped he was adopted – but I feared the worst. Needing to know what had become of Wally, I contacted the shelter director, Martha Wittkowski, who sadly informed me that Wally had passed away.

Encouraged by Wally, I confessed to Martha that I was a Reiki practitioner and wanted very much to work more with animals. We set up a time to meet, and I became a volunteer Reiki provider at Animal Lifeline, blocking out hours every other Saturday to work with the dogs and cats who were sick, depressed, recovering from surgery, or preparing to make their transition.

I do a lot of one-on-one work with the animals in a conference room housing a memorial area for animals who have crossed over. Sitting near the urns of ashes, surrounded by photographs and mementoes and tokens of love, the animal spirits gather near when I offer healing, lending their energy and offering their support. Central among these is Wally, the self-appointed Guardian Spirit of Animal Lifeline who reminds me, "The animals need you," and watches over the treatments with gentle satisfaction.

One afternoon, an animal caregiver who had been especially attached to Wally stood near Wally's ashes and memory objects while discussing his days at the shelter. I saw the speckled, shimmering image of an energy being hovering behind her left shoulder, and I knew this to be Wally, still actively participating in shelter life.

To Wally goes the credit for my being at Animal Lifeline. Through his story and his powerful spirit, he reached out, and in his search for an animal helper, he brought me. Every Reiki treatment I give at the shelter, every hug and kiss, and every heart-to-heart connection with an animal is a memorial to Wally – part of his living legacy of love and care for the people and animals at the place that became, for one sick dog, a brief taste of Paradise.

Animals and their Divine Guardians

Divine Source: God personally intervenes to heal and assist animals. I have seen and experienced this in very powerful ways. Awestruck, I asked, "Jesus, how can I make people understand that You are a direct Healer of animals?" He replied, "Just tell them."

So here is a story about a beautiful, sweet, four-year-old hound dog mix whose future hung in the balance due to a severe anxiety and panic disorder which was placing him and other animals in danger. Both he and the people who cared for him were in a miserable, heartbreaking situation as he jumped through windows, loosened steel bolts to escape from kennels, and shredded an electrical system as he tried to eat and claw his way through a wall.

When I was first asked to help him, we had a peaceful, hands-on session in which he deeply relaxed, showed much affection, and was finally able to eat his breakfast with a good appetite. However, he had been unable to hold the healthier vibration, and three days later conducted another dramatic and frenzied escape which left him bloodied and devastated.

Reaching out to him again, I did a distance Reiki session which I chose to perform during a walking meditation as it was a beautiful sunny day. A big dog, nearing 100 pounds, he wanted to be held like a baby which I could do easily in spirit. I immediately sensed that his heart center was the source of much pain and emotional baggage for him. I had expected to perhaps work with his brain and his brow chakra, but it was his heart that needed the work.

I saw a vision of a dry, black, desiccated structure, like a dehydrated and lifeless shell where his healthy, beating heart should have been. I was greatly stricken by this and was unsure of what to do. A powerful Spirit Guide stood back hesitantly when I asked for her help. I then called out, "Jesus," and He came at once, immediately stepping in to perform the work that was needed.

I saw a vision of Him blowing into the empty, hollow chambers of the deadened heart with the pranic breath of life, blowing out dust and debris which shimmered into nonexistence as the energetic tissues began to revive and restore. The black shell slowly became pink and alive, filled with prana as a physical heart would fill with blood. He told me to blow energetic breaths also, and so I did. This heart was literally resurrected from the dead.

When the energetic heart had enlivened, Jesus then took my hands and said, "Now the Reiki." Placing His hands over mine around the vision of this dog's heart, we sent the Reiki vibration of love. We also sent Reiki directly into the heart chakra, and I saw this structure as a spiral of light. I asked if I might see the chakra in more detail and was permitted to look into a geometric, grid-like structure, in the center of which were powerful, spinning lights – though I was cautioned not to "get lost" in this vision of the chakra.

Imagery of beautiful, dark pink roses began to bloom in the fertile spaces of this renewed heart, and I understood these roses as a symbol for Mother Mary, that the dog was being placed into her care. When His work for the moment was completed, Jesus left as swiftly as He had come, rushing upwards and out of the Reiki-linked energy fields of the dog and I, and the flow of energy abruptly ended. This was so disorienting, I was careful not to fall on the sidewalk!

This dog began a healing process at a profound spiritual level. Thanks to this Divine intervention, the medications to treat his anxiety and depression have begun to take hold. The sun is beginning to shine on his future, and with more Reiki and other help from Spirit, I am hopeful that his future will be bright indeed.

Angels and Ascended Masters: If one accepts animals as beings of Divine spirit, then it is logical to believe that animals have Guardian Angels just as people do. When I have worked with very sick cats and dogs and those who are transitioning out of life in the physical body, I have called upon Angelic helpers and have been aware of their protective presences around the animal. I have also received immediate and loving responses when asking for Angels to assist in shepherding an animal's soul as his physical body dies, and I even received a vision of Mother Mary holding and comforting a terminally ill dog. There is no doubt in my mind that animals are helped by Angels.

Just as all human being have at least two Guardian Angels protecting them, so all the Earth's creatures possessing the spirit of Godspark have Angelic guardians. Archangel Raphael has a tender concern for animals, and Archangel Michael is as much their protector as he is ours. Many believe that Faeries are the particular Earth Angels of the Nature Kingdom, and I have sometimes seen angels appear in a Faery-like, petite, delicate form with iridescent wings like a dragonfly.

Archangel Raphael is the supreme healing Angel. He wants us to know that his healing help is as close as our own hearts whenever we reach out to another living creature with the loving desire to help. His energetic manifestation is emerald green, a color principally associated with the heart chakra, and indeed, all healing energy is channeled through the heart and empowered by its love and purity.

Archangel Raphael particularly assists animals who are lost or homeless. I remember a worrisome midnight when my three big dogs went out and discovered another dog in our backyard, a small, tricolored beagle. He was thrilled to see my boys and played with them happily, though he shied away and ran from every attempt at human contact. With no collar or tags, it was impossible to know his circumstances.

At 1:15 a.m., after tracking him through several backyards, I had lost all trace of him. I could only send out Reiki for comfort with the message that I wanted to help him. I prayed to God and Archangel Raphael to please protect this little one and asked Raphael to either see him safely back to his home or return him to me.

At 6:00 a.m., my husband cried out, "He's back!" This time, with the assistance of our playful dogs and a bag of canine cookies, we managed to gain hold of him. Later that morning, after a call to a friend at a no-kill animal shelter, the little dog was cared for, neutered, and eventually reunited with his family. I believe that he was guided to our backyard by Archangel Raphael who had compassion for this sweet little spirit and brought him to a dog-loving place of rescue.

I frequently work with both Michael and Raphael together. Archangel Michael is a master at extracting negative energy structures and severing unhealthy connections while Archangel Raphael steps in to minister to the wounded areas. Archangel Michael is the supreme Angelic defender and champion of the besieged, and he will lead armies of Angels to protect and assist you and your animals from dangers both spiritual and material.

Archangel Ariel is an overlighting presence for all the Nature Kingdom, and she is sometimes called The Lioness of God. When I ask for her help with an animal, I frequently experience the healing energy of Archangel Ariel as a golden light that is accompanied by a feeling of feminine love and maternal tenderness. This occurs like rivers of sunlight pouring down from the heavens into the energetic and physical body of the animal in need, bringing deep calm and amplifying the healing work of Reiki, crystals, color therapy, and other dynamic modalities.

Most mysterious perhaps is The Guardian of Souls whom I

describe in the section about animals in the afterlife. It would appear that animals have a spiritual mother in this being much as humans do in Mother Mary, although I have also seen Mary herself provide nurture to animals as well as safe passage of their souls. Another figure who appeared to me prominently when I first began my spiritual work was the Black Madonna whom I would see holding the Christchild. The Black Madonna is a representative of the complex natures of the Divine Feminine, including the Blessed Virgin and more cryptically The Magdalene, and I believe that she symbolizes the feminine face of God.

Several metaphysicians, including a shamanic animal healer and a psychic medium, told me that St. Francis of Assisi wished to join me in my work with animals. An animal communicator received the message from him that, if I should become overwhelmed by an animal's grief, St. Francis stood ready to assist me. The first time I worked with a puppy mill survivor, shaking violently and terrified of human contact, I remembered this advice and asked both St. Francis and Archangel Ariel to help. The balanced combination of masculine and feminine energies as they worked in concert for the little dog was a powerful medicine.

Discarnate Souls: It is also possible to call on the souls of loved ones on the Other Side to assist with our animals. Another Reiki Master and I have each been assisted by our fathers who have acted as Guardian Spirits and helpers of animals who are ill or hospitalized, suffering in similar circumstances to what each of these men went through during their final physical struggles. A heartfelt plea for assistance is all that is needed to engage the spiritual help and cooperation of our predeceased loved ones. They are quite willing and capable to work with us if we call on them.

The souls of many deceased animals are also very eager to help their animal brethren in Physical Reality. I have experienced deceased animal souls returning to the remaining animals in their pack to bring spiritual calm and guidance as the new pack order becomes established. These disincarnate animal spirits may remain with the family for some time, acting as a spiritual pack leader and helper.

I have also worked with the souls of several dogs and cats who return to assist dying animals in their soul transition process, greeting and welcoming them to the Spiritual Realm. Other animal spirits participate in healing sessions as comforters or remain by the side of a distressed animal in need of their companionship. Just as human souls do, animal souls take up a variety of work when they transition out of the physical body – and they invite us to call upon them now, just as we would have called to them in earthly life.

Angel Case Study: Oscar

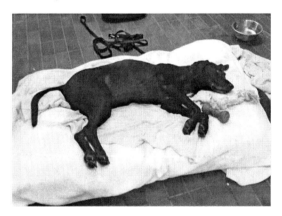

Oscar is a special dog, one of those creatures with whom I had an immediate heart connection. I first met him, a black and brown Labrador Retriever/Bloodhound mix, when he was brought from Avondale Animal Hospital to Animal Lifeline of Iowa after his people relinquished him, and I was asked to perform a Reiki treatment. He was completely paralyzed, stricken with Coonhound paralysis, usually a temporary condition, though it can last for many months. Only seven years old when his people opted to euthanize him because

they couldn't afford his care, he was saved by a kindhearted veterinarian and the willing hearts at a small, special-needs animal shelter.

After my first session with Oscar, during which he lay motionless on a mattress, only able to turn his head and unable even to lift it, I told the shelter director that I would provide some extra sessions for him. I returned in three days, and Oscar's condition was largely unchanged. He was in fairly good spirits, and other than some wasting of his large muscles, he looked healthy. Toward the end of the week, he would have his first treatment on the underwater treadmill at the veterinary clinic.

When I returned four days later on a Saturday afternoon, his condition had markedly deteriorated. Atrophied and wasted, he looked like a skeleton in a dog skin, and he whimpered and cried in pain, deep sores like open sacks on both hips, both shoulders, and one elbow. I lay down with Oscar in his bloody bedding and cried as I held him. The animal caregiver on duty was also brought to tears by this dog's suffering.

The staff told me that Oscar had finally gotten some return of movement in his trunk. Flopping like a seal, he was dragging himself around his room at the shelter and even getting down the hallway. His zeal to move had torn open his flesh where the bones projected so pitifully in his wasted frame. To prevent further injuries, it was decided to place him in a kennel with an E-collar on whenever no one could stay in the room with him.

The wounds were flushed several times daily, packed with ointment, and dressed. Additional pain medications were added to his regimen, and concerned staff watched over him. He even received veterinarian "house-calls" at the shelter. Still, Oscar was experiencing great pain and suffering. As I propped him on his back to take pressure off his wounds, supporting him with pillows and towel rolls, his brown eyes looked up at me, filled with fear, and his breathing was hard.

I offered Oscar Reiki and used a technique the Tibetan Buddhists call Tonglen which uses the breath as a conduit for suffering. An empathetic healing practice, I used Tonglen to take Oscar's pain and affliction into my own body and then expel it from myself in a way that would ground and transmute the negative energies. My throat and upper airways ached with a dull scraping pain afterwards where Oscar's suffering had been borne in on my breath. I had not envisioned ever having the courage to try such a practice, but at the sight of Oscar, I had used it immediately.

I called all of my Lightworker friends, and together we poured out Reiki, prayers, healing energy, shamanic journeys, sacred drumming and drum healing, and everything else we could muster. My friend Alan did a powerful, two-hour shamanic healing journey for Oscar and told me that he had extracted a lot of thick, murky energy with a consistency of pudding which he felt was the energy of the disease that had caused the paralysis, making Oscar's body stagnant. He was assisted by Power Animals, Spirit Guides, and other beings and was instructed in retrieving spirit medicine to revitalize Oscar.

Alan transported Oscar's soul to his crystal "operating room" where he does his healing work, and at the end of the session, Oscar did not want to return to his body because of the pain and suffering there. He wasn't ready to transition, but he went back reluctantly. Alan said, "He's half in and half out of the door" but not yet ready to

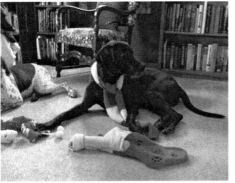

discuss euthanasia. He also cautioned about a great risk for infection.

Grateful for Alan's work and insights, I was devastated to hear of Oscar's severe depression and that he was losing the will to live. I did a meditation/prayer ses-

sion that night, calling upon Jesus and Archangel Raphael to work urgently with Oscar. I asked for assistance from all of my Power Animals, Spirit Guides, and Guardian Angels, as well as Archangel Ariel. I felt a swift and strong response, and I envisioned Archangel Raphael's emerald green light filling Oscar's deep wounds, forming new tissue to heal them, and coursing through his bloodstream to invigorate his body. I pictured Jesus and Raphael working together as they placed their healing hands on Oscar.

When I opened my eyes, the angle of the partly open door in my Reiki treatment room placed a huge cross outlined in light directly in front of my eyes. This was very reassuring, and I looked at this image for a long time and asked again what I could do. I was told clearly that I had done all I could do, and it was now in the hands of Jesus and the Angels. They were taking it from there.

My husband, a nurse, went to see Oscar the next morning and performed all of his wound care, telling me that there were no signs of infection and the wounds looked serious but something from which Oscar could recover. He sounded encouraging, but I was still nervous. When I got to the shelter that night, however, and saw Oscar for myself, what met my eyes was nothing short of a miracle.

Oscar's body was actually more robust and larger, something that was medically "impossible" after just forty-eight hours in a dog who couldn't move. His pain was controlled, he was in good spirits, and he happily ate the turkey and ham I brought him. He even had a trace of movement in his back legs, was able to raise and turn his head, turn himself over, and stretch out his front legs and push against me with his foot, providing resistance. He was simply not the same dog. He was a dog who had been restored, who knew many people were working on his behalf, and who had felt the touch of the Divine.

I fell in love with Oscar at first sight and knew that he belonged with me. More than that, I recognized him as part of an old soul grouping connected to me, and I recalled a past lifetime with him. (These memories were later confirmed in detail by an independent medium).

Much to the surprise of many, my husband and I immediately began the adoption process. However he would finally recover, we loved Oscar and we wanted him. Within eight weeks, Oscar was standing and taking a few steps on his own, progress that our veterinarian (who had treated three other dogs with this disease) felt was incredible, stating that it normally took twelve weeks to see even minor improvements.

As he recovered, I asked Oscar if he wanted to come home with me. He said that he did, and that he envisioned my home as being a quiet haven where he could spend his "retirement." He was nervous about learning the layout of the house and was unsure what his role in the family would be, so we arranged a number of home visits in addition to play dates at the shelter for Oscar and his new brothers.

In late fall of 2011, Oscar starred in a television spot about Oscar the Wonder Dog. He was the guest of honor at the Paws and Claws Benefit Auction for Animal Lifeline, decked out in his formalwear of a vest and bowtie, and helped raise record funds. He was also featured in at least two periodicals including a veterinary medicine publication.

On October 29, 2011, Oscar officially joined our family, steadfastly walking into his forever home to stay. A former "outside dog," Oscar has taken easily and happily to his indoor life with his family. He has bonded with his dog brothers and found a place for himself in the new pack structure.

By January 2012, six months after he fell ill, Oscar was running and jumping, playing with his brothers, guarding his new home, and curling up in bed with Mommy, Daddy, Reggie, and Jack. His flaky skin had grown smooth, his thin and profusely shedding coat was thick and soft, and his gentle and sweet temperament never left him.

He requires thick boots and a winter coat when he goes out in the snow, suffering from cold-induced neuropathic pain in his feet and having lost his resistance to cold weather. He's also the first to tire in the heat, wanting the comfort of a soft bed and air conditioning. A profoundly loving dog, he gets all the pampering he could want!

Oscar inspires us daily. He passed through his dark night of the soul and determined that he would see the sun again. He never gave up on his goal of returning to wholeness. First wiggling a foot, and then flopping, turning, crawling, and finally sitting, standing, and at last walking again, he charted a steady course through the darkness. One look at his face will tell you that, despite his moments of fear and cries of frustration, he never truly doubted his triumphant outcome of healing. He even joins me occasionally in sending healing Reiki treatments to other dogs, helping me connect and communicate.

Still in shock at his circumstances when I met him at the shelter, Oscar wondered why this had happened to him. The answer I received for him was that he was being taught a lesson in humility. A powerful dog, accustomed to a commanding presence and dominion over all the creatures in his environment, he had been felled so that he might learn what it meant to be helpless. In a strange place, he was dependent on others for hand feeding and drinking through a bulb syringe because he couldn't raise his head. He had to be turned on his mattress several times a day and have his limbs put through range of motion and his body massaged. He was carried outside to eliminate.

He learned the necessity for mercy, he learned to be humble, and he learned what a loving bond with a human could mean. He learned to persevere in the present and hope for the future. Then, when he had mastered these lessons, he taught them to the rest of us.

Angel Case Study: Nim

I was first contacted about a little cat called Nim when a volunteer at the shelter told the director that Nim "had some demons around her" but that she had been able to "make some of them go away." Deeply concerned not only for Nim but for the other animals and people at the shelter, I considered the case an emergency.

Nim was returned to the shelter after spending almost her whole three years in one home. Her caretakers explained that she had become aggressive towards them and towards the other cat in the home. Their veterinarian had prescribed Prozac which did not help. Afraid that a serious injury would occur, ultimately her caretakers made the decision to relinquish Nim back to the shelter.

My first action was to go into a state of meditation in which I could consult with the highest-level spiritual beings regarding any evil influences on the cat and the possible need for a clearing or exorcism. All of the information I received about Nim's case came to me remotely from this session. I specifically called upon Jesus Christ, Archangel Michael, and Archangel Raphael to show me what was wrong with Nim and how to go about fixing it.

I was told that in fact there were no demons or evil spirits plaguing this animal. She had what is sometimes referred to as an "energy shackle" around her head. Energy shackles represent deep emotions and patterns of behavior that are presenting in the energy field of the person/animal. This energetic manifestation is what leads to physical symptoms of pain, illness, et cetera. Energy shackles in people are always related to feelings of powerlessness, confinement, oppression, or feelings of victimization. In people, these are sometimes seen around the neck in someone who has been in a controlling, abusive relationship. They can appear as a yoke on the shoulders of someone who is over-burdened, often one who takes on other people's problems as well as their own. Different types of fear are generally at the root of these negative energy forms.

Nim's energy shackle appeared to me with the symbolism of a crown of thorns or a tiara of long thorns, very torturing to wear. A crown of thorns makes a mockery out of sovereignty – in this case, Nim's personal sovereignty and Higher Self identity. Underneath this, I was shown bleeding wounds, holes in her energy field. When I asked what caused this, I saw one of the yin/yang symbols. It was stretched and elongated and warped out of shape, and its counterpart was missing.

Everyone is comprised of opposing forces that react to each other – yin/yang, masculine/feminine, light/dark, et cetera. In Nim's case, these energies were fundamentally unbalanced, and this was partially causative of her problems. Such an imbalance could have been triggered by a physical or emotional trauma, a long or difficult illness, or some other disruption in her life.

Her true nature and essence as Nim the Cat had been repressed or somehow turned against her or been made into a mockery. Since her shackles and wounds were centered around Nim's head, these energetic manifestations showed up in her body as emotional/psychological/behavioral issues regarding her brain.

The most important things to do were to remove the energy shackle, heal the wounds in her energy field, and restore her energetic system to its proper balance. These were the goals of our initial session, and I felt that she would need extra care and a time of convalescence. I had asked if the treatment could be done right away remotely, but it was impressed upon me that this initial work needed to be done in her physical presence. I feel that much of the reason for this was because these great beings wished to use this opportunity to educate me in these matters so that I may become an able assistant for them and teach others about such things

I asked what I needed to do to protect myself, and I was told to travel light, taking only what I needed and not burdening myself with *what was unnecessary. Most especially, I was instructed to choose my traveling companions well – in this case Jesus, Michael, and Raphael.*

Nim was ready to release this negative energy, and so the treatment itself was actually very easy. Taking only thirty minutes, it was rather anti-climactic, but my Reiki Master explained that this was due to the fact that much had already been done through the preparatory work. I brought my Reiki stones to arrange in an altar, and I brought two large quartz points (one masculine and one feminine) to put on either side of Nim's body as I channeled Reiki. I used a piece of kyanite between her shoulders for chakra balancing, and I did crystal wand massage with selenite to detoxify and replenish her and banish negativity from her energy field. My kyanite is shaped like an arrow, and I felt guided to use the point to cut away etheric patterns around her head to facilitate removal of the shackle. Afterwards, Archangel Raphael placed a temporary green-light healing structure on and around her head to continue his work.

This "violent" cat purred and rubbed her head into my hands. This "scared" cat who'd been cowering in her condo shook herself all over after the treatment, indicated she was ready for her fresh start, and started exploring the cat room. (I had been cautioned that she probably wouldn't come out of the condo). Clearly, animals have a lot less difficulty letting go of their old baggage — fewer psychological devices and conflicting inner voices cluttering up the works and hiding the truth.

By her second Reiki session, she had been seen lounging on the top berth of her cat condo, a sign of increased confidence. Again, she burrowed her head eagerly into my hands and went into a deep Reiki sleep. During her treatment, she indicated that her former caretakers had been boisterous and her home had been loud, and she had indeed disliked the other resident cat. The noise and activity level had been too stressful for her, and she showed me a disturbing image of the other cat looming over and bullying her.

I asked her to start thinking and dreaming about "Nim's Ideal Home" so that we could begin making this a reality for her. She em-

phasized that she would like a quiet home with low-key people and soft voices and needed a peaceful environment. Always very sweet when I worked with her, I didn't see the aggression her former family talked about. I think that the situation in that home was just hard on her nerves. In many ways, she found being at the shelter a relief, a reprieve from something she couldn't handle.

A quiet, sensitive cat, she had been freed from a lot of emotional baggage, a bad reputation, and the frustration of being repeatedly misunderstood. With the help of God and the Angelic Realm, Nim was well on her way to a new and satisfying life.

We learned later that, after adopting a kitten to replace Nim, her former people realized that the underlying behavior problem was with their other cat all along, just as Nim had shown me. In January 2012, Nim was happily adopted into her forever home, together with another feline friend from the shelter. She continues to thrive.

Angel Healing for Animals

Guided visualization for invoking Angelic assistance for our animal companions

When the animals we love are sick or afraid, we are seized with the same urge to help that we feel when any of our beloved are in need. Rest assured that no ailment or trouble is too vast or too insignificant for you to call upon Angelic beings who in fact are prepared at all times to minister to the needs of you and your loved ones.

Sit quietly with the spirit of the dog, cat, horse, or other animal being for whom you wish healing and comfort. This may be your own animal companion or that of a friend. Hold this animal close in thought. You may choose to seek healing for all suffering animals, or all those waiting in shelters. Picture them now. Your animal may be held in your arms or on your lap, but if not, cradle him or her close with your spiritual arms, reaching out with your heart to draw near to the animal's precious essence.

Anyone can converse with the Angels, including animals, for Angels are with us always, eternally within our reach. We need only to call upon them, for they will never violate any being's free will and only act when they are summoned.

Breathe deeply, in and out of your heart center, the in-breath filling the heart chakra with an ever expanding light, a glowing mist of soft green and rose pink that spirals in the turning rhythm of this energy center. As you enliven the heart chakra and its beams of light radiate out in front and behind, let the out-breath flow the radiance out into your aura, pink and green moonbeams and sun rays that surround your whole being in a shimmering halo of loving light.

Imagine your aura wrapping itself into an orb of light, like you're inside a crystal sphere that shifts effortlessly between rose quartz and peridot, pink tourmaline and emerald, jade and clear quartz, like a captured moonbeam. In this bright circle of light you hold your beloved animal or animals, suspended together in your crystal space.

Call now to Divine Source by whatever name is known to your heart, and call upon the White Light Beings of the Angelic Realms, call upon your Guardian Angels, and Spirit Guides, Power Animals, and whatever spiritual helpers you would like to join you. They may surround you in the ethers in your quiet place, or you may invite them into your light sphere, your crystal globe that you now bless together and consecrate to a work of healing, a sacred space.

Call upon the Most High to empower this healing effort for your beloved animal. *Divine Healer, Jesus Christ, I call upon you now for your merciful healing power to be bestowed upon* _____. (Say the name of the animal here, or the group of animals, the shelter, or however you identify them and the place where they are). *I ask that you summon all appropriate Angelic healers and Divine Spirits to surround and strengthen* _____ *according to the needs both known and unknown to me.*

Know that God is with you, that He answers swiftly and with gentle strength, bringing with Him a whole illuminated host of Angels. Allow yourself to feel their peaceful energy suffusing you with comfort and assurance that you and your loved one are in the best of hands.

Reach out now to Archangel Raphael, the powerful Celestial Healer, with a simple invocation. *Archangel Raphael, I need your help and ask you with a free will and an open heart to bring a miracle of healing for* _____ , *to work in your wisdom for this creature's highest good, and to heal and restore in mind, body, and spirit. Please come to* _____ *and place your healing hands upon* his/her *body, filling this beloved creature with your wise and loving light to energize and heal, relieve pain and suffering, and bring comfort and total wellbeing.*

See the Archangel, a serene and merciful power who brings with him an emerald green radiance of Divine heart light and healing love. Invite him to join you and your animal loved one in your crystal sphere, the emerald atmosphere of his healing energy bathing you completely in its glowing beams. His face is loving and his aspect is one of Divine power, empathy, and mercy.

Watch him pour his light like a shimmering green water into any wounds, any organs of the body that are sick. See its crystalline brilliance transmuting all negative energies trapped in the animal's body, opening up channels for healing to flow freely, its bright current washing away impurities and disease.

What is your animal telling you at this time? Are you feeling old, stuck emotions of sadness or grief or fear as the animal expresses and releases these blockages? Are you feeling sensations in your body that correspond to the sick places in your animal's body?

Be still, and if you can, rest your hands lightly on your animal's body – or else you can do this by intention. You may feel a humming, high-energy vibration which is Archangel Raphael's healing work taking place. You might feel this through your hands where they rest on the animal, or you may feel it in your heart center or throughout your body.

As the Angels finish their work, you will feel a peaceful glow all around you. You may see your animal bathed in a golden light or cradled lovingly in Angelic arms. You may hear the beating of wings and feel a breeze move across your skin.

Offer up thanks from your heart to your God, Archangel Raphael, and any other Angels or Guides who have taken part in the healing. Thank your animal for being a receptive vessel for the Divine healing power. Be humbled as a creature of the Earth who has been cared for by celestial hands. Feel the powerful energy of the Divine love for you and your animal companions which is present in all the earthly and cosmic forms that are lit from within by the Universal Life Force Energy we share. As you breathe in and out, letting the energy flow in all its natural channels, and allowing your crystal sphere to disperse like a jade-colored cloud back into your aura, know that this place of healing awaits you and your loved ones – animal or human – at all times, and that you may be joined here by the Angels whenever their presence is needed. Breathe in and out through the heart chakra, breathing love and the deepest sense of wellbeing, secure in knowing that the vast powers of Spirit are with you and the creatures of the Earth in burrows and dens, nests and living rooms, and animal shelters. Your animals know that you and they are never alone.

Below is part of a grid from a Crystal and Angelic Reiki session I performed for an animal soul transition.

Index of Angels, Ascended Masters, and Spiritual Beings Who Work with Animals

- **Archangel Ariel** – The Lioness of God, she is an over-lighting Angelic Being for all of the Nature Kingdom including animals, minerals and crystals, plants, the Earth, and the environment. Her healing energy comes on a golden wave like the sun and induces great peace.

- **Archangel Gabriel** – This Archangel facilitates inter-species communication as well as access to the Akashic Records. He can be called upon to assist animals with throat chakra issues and can help misunderstood animals to express themselves to their human caretakers.

- **Archangel Michael** – The supreme protector of the Angelic Realm, he provides guardianship and defense of animals and their people. He also performs powerful healing work in cutting away and banishing negative energy patterns and entities.

- **Archangel Raphael** – He is the ultimate healing Angel and works to disarm all forms of dis-ease at the spiritual, physical, mental, and emotional levels. He also shepherds and helps lost animals.

- **Buddha** – Ascended Master and Avatar of Vishnu (the Hindu deity whom many equate with the True God of Judaism and Christianity), he is a compassionate friend to animals. All animals possess Buddha nature and the ability to achieve Enlightenment, and Buddha is a wise teacher both to animals and their humans regarding life on Earth and the ultimate journey of the soul.

- **Guardian Angels of the individual animal** – Each creature on Earth has one or more Guardian Spirits who can be called on directly to assist with that animal's health, wellbeing, and protection. You may choose to ask your own Guardian Angels to communicate with or assist the Guardian Angels of your animal companion. It is also possible to send Reiki energy to strengthen an animal's Guardian Angels in times of trouble or distress.

- **The Guardian of Souls** – This mystical primordial being assists animals at the time of transition from incarnated life in a physical body to Light in the Spiritual Realm. An ancient nature spirit, she has a connection to the Divine Feminine.

- **Jesus Christ** – Ascended Master and Avatar of the True God, Jesus is an energetic link to Source for humans and animals. He pours forth His fount of healing waters in the form of Reiki energy which is brought to animals by attuned human Reiki channels. He also performs direct healing miracles upon animals and answers every call for help. Jesus is an all-powerful Protector in the face of negative energies or entities, easily deconstructing and exorcising such forms. When there is ever a doubt about how to proceed or guidance seems unclear, call upon Jesus for Divine discernment and knowledge.

- **Kwan Yin** – The Bodhisattva of Compassion, this Buddhist goddess brings healing love, comfort, and supportive energy to all species of animals and their people. Her presence is accompanied by a menagerie of animal spirits who offer their own assistance.

- **Mother Mary** – The Divine Feminine Mother for human

beings, she also showers her love and compassionate care on members of the Animal Kingdom. It seems to be a function of Divine Feminine nurture to aid the souls of departing animals. When asked for help, Mother Mary lovingly guards and cares for them in her Divine embrace.

- **Saint Francis of Assisi** – St. Francis preached the Gospel to animals as his own brothers and sisters. He is a ready helper for animals who are suffering or grieving, offering comfort, healing, and prayer. He also supports and assists people who work with animals, offering his strength in trying times.

- **Saint Joseph** – The husband of Mother Mary, St. Joseph appears to assist animals in need of extra protection. He is a paternal figure, offering guardianship, strength, and watchful love to animals who are particularly vulnerable. I have seen him working in concert with Jesus Christ and Mother Mary.

- **The Tree Being** – This ancient and mysterious being seems to be a Divine Masculine spirit of the Elemental Kingdom. He is present to assist with soul transitions of animals. He also serves to remind us to keep hold of wonder and to look beyond the surface appearance of things.

Why We Should Care

W e live in a world of form where life is precarious and our bodies are more fragile than the souls within them. Humans are gradually remembering a truth that animals have always known – that this Physical Reality of form fosters a grand illusion of separateness and isolation. We are all truly parts of a Divine Whole. We are each part of one another.

An orthodox view of our situation might be that, since the primordial time of the Fall, humans have sought desperately to distance themselves from the rest of the created world, claiming separate and elevated status from all other life forms. This quest to prove and enforce a regime of human superiority is a direct response to (or perhaps the cause of) our expulsion from Paradise – the time when we lived in harmony with all species of living creatures and existed in a state of blissful Unity with the Divine.

A more Gnostically-influenced interpretation – and the one which resonates with me – is that humans were not the enemy who, by the work of Eve, cast a pall over the entire course of human history and blighted the creation. Instead, the creation itself is flawed, the work of lesser deities than the Divine Source from whom the substance of creation emanated. We inhabit a world that is often unjust and cruel. Rather than trying to rationalize unfairness and evil as somehow either a loving God's harsh will or the inheritance of human wickedness, we can accept evil on its face and know that it does not in fact come from God but from the flawed workings of the lower beings (the Demiurge and the archons) who created with God's substance.

A Gnostic-inspired view continues that the spirits in all incarnated beings are filled with the Godspark of the True God, and we struggle in the created Universe to remember who and what we truly are and to find our way upward to wisdom and filial existence with the Divine. This is where animals assist humans with their native intuitive wisdom about our true Source and nature. It is essential therefore, to remember that this climb back to a communion with the Divine must include *all* the soul beings with which we share the world – animals and humans together.

We live in a time when the material, created world is regarded by many as "all that is," and a mission to dominate Physical Reality is paramount for many people. Our society is also influenced by a number of traditions that have attempted to bestow on human beings a singular or dominant right to exist and thrive and an exclusive lock on being "children of God." However, it is our very forgetfulness of and distance from the true nature of Divinity as it resides, scattered throughout the creation, which has led to humankind's bloody quest for world domination.

This quest has taken many distasteful forms over the course of human history. People of color, Jews, women, homosexuals, Native Americans, and persons with disabilities have all felt the blunt end of the "superiority" stick as humans have squabbled even amongst our own species to establish and enforce artificial linear hierarchies of supremacy. We live in a time of greater Enlightenment than previous generations, and we can be rightfully pleased with the growing climate of acceptance among people. However, the work must not end there.

Animals are the last broad category of beings on the Earth over whom humans claim the ultimate dominance. This phony claim of dominance is as fallacious as the despicable lies that Jews are a subhuman species or that epileptics are possessed by the Devil. It is, in fact, part of the final illusion that keeps humanity out of Eden, which is not a place from which humans were expelled but a place before and beyond creation to which all souls must aspire to return.

Today, in laboratories all over America, animals are suffering in cages, deliberately infected with diseases, injected with drugs, poisoned, tortured, and killed in the name of "scientific advancement." One must only think of the primates who were permanently blinded after their eyelids were sewn shut for protracted periods to "study" the effects of visual deprivation. "The rabbit died" is still a trite little quip to signal a human pregnancy, hearkening back to the not-so-distant time when a new human life was heralded by the killing of an animal. The name "guinea pig" is synonymous with a hapless creature used for experiments, and drug companies abuse animals routinely as part of their "product demonstrations" at medical conventions.

Why is animal spirituality important? As we explore the root chakra and journey deeper into this energy center, we learn about our connection to and deep roots within the Earth. We discover that, just as our Higher Consciousness/Soul Body are created by our Cosmic Father, so our physical bodies are born from the body of our Earth Mother, the feminine nature of God's energies which allowed for the creation of physical forms and physical worlds. These vehicles in which our Higher Consciousness may have experiences in physicality are of the same substance as the Earth and are anchored in her to make possible our existence in the plane of Physical Reality.

Animals also have consciousness as is illustrated by their emotional reactions, feelings such as loyalty and love, their cooperation in family groups such as wolf packs or whale pods, acts of selflessness and altruism, and their needs for communication and companionship. They too have physical bodies crafted from and rooted in the body of the Earth and Soul Bodies emanated from our Creator Source. We share with them the same Parents. We are their family.

Learning to understand and appreciate the other forms of embodied consciousness on our planet gives us multiple perspectives from which to comprehend our place in the Universe and discover the truths which we are here to find. Loving the Animal Kingdom is a lesson in humility for human beings, self-styled as "the dominant species" or "superior beings." The great hope is that we learn to use our powers judiciously, perhaps even turning our prowess for killing into a talent for nurture and our "Divine Right of Kings" mentality into a zest for preservation and sharing of the Earth's bounty which is intended for all the life forms she has incubated.

Why is a metaphysical study of animals relevant? Astrologers tell us that the Age of Aquarius is dawning, and part of the birth pangs of the New Age is the repayment of karmic debt which has accumulated over the hundreds of centuries of the dying age. This karmic retribution can be seen in so-called "Biblical" floods like the tsunamis that have devastated Asia, massive earthquakes, hurricanes like Katrina which have laid waste to our high tech cities, and plagues such as influenza pandemics or AIDS. At a Reiki workshop I attended in 2010, the Master declared that the Earth was fighting back after generations of waste and pollution and human arrogance.

This Earth who is fighting back with the accumulated karma of millennia is not the sole province of humanity. Our actions take a toll on all with whom we share the planet – perhaps most deeply on the Animal Kingdom which has seen so many species become extinct while countless more struggle to survive on smaller and smaller allotments of habitat in the face of human encroachment.

If humanity is to succeed in achieving the potential for Higher Consciousness which is becoming possible now, it is essential that we first begin to comprehend the interconnectedness of Being. Wars would not be fought if we truly understood what is meant by the words "The Brotherhood (and Sisterhood) of Man," that *this* inseparable connection of all humanity past and present is what Christ meant when He spoke of The Golden Rule and taught, "That which you do to the least of these, you do to Me."

Animals would no longer be tortured to death in laboratories or callously dumped into raging rivers if we realized that this connectivity extends to *all* life under the heavens of our Cosmic Father and in the bosom of our Earth Mother. Christ, born in a manger in the company of animals, called Himself both The Good Shepherd and The Lamb of God. The Book of Revelation describes animals in Heaven and speaks of Christ returning to earth on a white horse. Civilizations from regions as diverse as Egypt and Mesoamerica speak of dogs as both the guardians and guides of human beings in the underworld or the afterlife. St. Francis preached the Gospel to animals. The Hindus have a vast pantheon of animal gods as do many other religions. Buddha taught that animals are possessed of Buddha nature and have the same opportunity to achieve Enlightenment as human beings.

Appreciation for and understanding of the Buddha nature of animals, of their possession of a soul and a Higher Consciousness, is a gateway for humanity to embrace Unity and love and strive to foster a peaceful Universe where all may blossom and fully awaken. Indeed, animals are one of our last connections to the sparsely-trodden path back to the Oneness of all creatures – animal, mineral, vegetation, and human – that we once enjoyed. Separateness is a function of the descent into the Universe of all beings, and animals have gone with us on this journey. By their loyalty and grace, however, they offer to help us climb back up together.

Case Studies in Abuse Recovery

In less than twelve months in 2011, I worked with two animals who were shot in the face at point-blank range. Lily was a pregnant

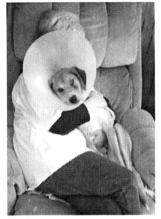

hound dog whose person took a rifle to her face and dumped her in a ditch to die with her unborn pups where she languished for two days. CJ is a sweet cat who was shot in the head and lost her left eye as a result. Yet, for each monster who victimized these sweet creatures, there are many more humans surrounding each of them with love.

A kindly man rescued Lily, and she gave birth at an animal sanctuary before coming to Animal Lifeline of Iowa to undergo numerous reconstructive surgeries. When I met her, shortly after one of several operations to remove teeth that had been pushed through her face, extract buckshot fragments, and close the skin, she was gentle and loving, ready to give humans another chance. She nuzzled into my lap, happy to be alive, giving out love with a seemingly boundless capacity. She is now in her forever home, sharing her great love with her new family.

When I first met CJ at the shelter, she rolled over and purred. She recovered well from the surgery to remove her shattered eye. Rehabilitated from her trauma, she learned to live with the partial loss of her vision. Now in her forever home, she is basking in the love of human companionship and care.

Neither Lily nor CJ was ruined by their horrific experiences at the hands of people. Their capacity to forgive, to give second and third and fourth chances, their zest for life, courage, undiminished spirits, and boundless love are unspeakably humbling. I have only to take one of these precious ones in my arms to know the beauty of God, to see the Divine spark alive and well inside these furry bodies.

Animals are humanity's way back into the sunshine of Enlight-

enment and the deep knowledge of the Divine. They beckon us every day – despite what so many of our kind have done to them.

We all know the words, *"To err is human, to forgive divine."* The faithful forgiveness of a dog abandoned on a highway or a pregnant cat thrown into a river is Divine. It is the God-nature of animals that speaks in this way – in short, their souls.

Modern humans, with their obsessive love for Western scientific thought and its flawed and disproven theses, have forgotten – even banished – the wisdom inherent in the natural world. The ancients knew that humans were part of the tapestry of Nature. Shamans and medicine people learned to merge with the spirits of their animal totems to invoke their energies and their wisdom. Early humans, even though they hunted for food, honored the sacrifices of the animals they killed, and provision was made for the animal soul.

As we look at the moral and spiritual bankruptcy of our modern world, people are increasingly turning away from the fads of the Scientific Revolution, and the ever-changing human-declared truths of expediency that have fostered so much bloodshed and misery. For an example of such heinous reasoning, one need only look to the wholesale slaughter of Native Americans and the erasing from the Earth of entire civilizations in the name of Manifest Destiny. What chance did animals have in a human society that preyed so ruthlessly on itself?

Today in Alaska, the aerial slaughter of wolves to maintain human supremacy in the region is being met with protest and outcry that would have been unthinkable 100 years ago. The Sea Shepherds risk their lives battling to stop illegal Japanese whaling. The America Society for the Prevention of Cruelty to Animals (ASPCA) and The Humane Society of the United States are widely-supported organizations which have counterparts operating in many countries. Puppy mills and dog-fighting rings are gradually being shut down. Progress is being made.

We are relearning ancient ways of respect for the Earth, seeing by the horrific examples of oil spills and radiation leaks that all life is interconnected. More and more private gardens and commercial farms are growing plants with organic methods. People are increasingly integrating a green lifestyle into their choice of building materials, cleaning products, and clothes. Solar panels and wind farms are generating environmentally-friendly power for large numbers of people.

Western medicine and veterinary science have certainly conveyed vast benefits on humans and animals, but more and more, people are rediscovering the natural and energetic modalities that complement and augment modern Western methods and can help uphold and sustain good health. As we begin to understand again the subtle bodies and the true causes of dis-ease, there is renewed interest in naturopathy, homeopathy, Reiki, osteopathy and chiropractic, reflexology, guided imagery, crystals, and prayer. These are the time-honored ways of creating harmony among the energetic bodies, fostering peace with self and the world, and gratefully accepting the abundant healing offered to our physical and subtle forms by Mother Earth who is our fount of nurturing sustenance.

Inherent in all this is appreciation for and interest in the natural world. We have begun to care again what animals, plants, the oceans and forests, the Earth and the Universe have to tell us. Astrologers teach that the Age of Aquarius is a time of rapid evolution for humanity as we attune to the higher-vibration energies which are bombarding the planet. It's a time of awakening for many people – a time that the Animal Kingdom has long awaited.

Franky, A Very Good Boy

The best way to sum-
marize this volume on
animal spirituality came to
me in the form of deep sessions I performed for an
ailing German Shorthaired
Pointer named Franky.
Found wandering with a col-
lar embedded in his neck, Franky had come to Animal Lifeline
four-and-a-half years earlier and had made the shelter his home.
For many people, Franky was synonymous with Animal Lifeline.
He was the first animal I ever met there, delivering Christmas
donations one cold December night in 2007.

Late in November 2011, the shelter contacted me to let me
know Franky was in the hospital with an attack of acute pancre-
atitis and was feeling quite low. I immediately resolved to do a
distance Reiki session for Franky who had taken Reiki from me
hands-on many times.

I called upon Jesus Christ, Lord of the Reiki, to send this
Living Water through me in abundance for Franky's healing.
Using rose quartz, silver topaz, and bloodstone, I enlisted my
Spirit Guide to gather and transmute whatever darkness was
released. Franky was present at once between my hands, coming through strongly across the energetic bridge. I performed
a wanding session with the bloodstone, aware of a deep space
opening up in Franky's energetic body over his thoracic spine,

like the flaps of a box folding back and revealing a depth of unhealthy energy. I held the wand like a wick and directed the dark and lurid-colored energies of illness and blockages up and out through the bloodstone.

Once this area was cleared, I sent Reiki to strengthen Franky's Angelic Guardians, asking them to come forward and protect what was still a gaping hole his energetic system. I became aware of a host of small, Faery-like Angels with beautiful iridescent blue wings like those of a dragonfly or a moth. Perhaps six in number, they huddled over Franky's body, spreading their wings and their arms to protect his vulnerable area with a living shield.

A Spirit Guide then performed a type of "psychic surgery" followed by a shamanic and primal sound healing, rhythmic vibrations dispersing the old etheric patterns and reshaping them, manifesting healing. This was a very significant spiritual event.

When I exchanged Reiki with my Guide, thanking her for helping Franky, the waves of energy were like golden flames blowing past my face and eyes and through my whole being. So many eternal beings such as Christ, Spirit Guides, Angels, and nature spirits would not concern themselves so intimately with physical bodies that were mere empty vessels. Rather, they were responding to assist the incarnated soul within Franky's body.

Let's examine that phrase "mere empty vessels." By definition, a vessel is a container. If we believe that human physical bodies are soul containers, why should animal bodies not be so? There are plenty of people who don't believe that *humans* have souls, discount "life after death" claims, and think that existence is confined to one physical lifetime. In such a climate of skepticism about all esoteric concepts, the realities of animal souls will take longer to be fully revealed and accepted as more people embark down their own paths of spiritual Enlightenment. However, I *know* that animals have souls. I have seen and communicated with them directly as have many other healers, psychic mediums, and animal lovers.

Sadly, we discovered shortly after the above treatment that Franky had inoperable cancer which had started in the bile duct and spread to his pancreas and liver. Franky deteriorated rapidly, losing weight and unwilling to eat, having difficulty standing, and becoming jaundiced. The shelter's director pledged that Franky would not be allowed to suffer.

Sooner than expected, it was determined that the kindest thing for Franky was to have him humanely euthanized. I arranged to be with Franky at the hospital so that I could provide this beloved dog with transitional assistance. This was a special privilege and not normally permitted, as even the most well-intentioned people can impede what is best and most peaceful for the animal. (Final goodbyes by numbers of people are best said in another setting if at all possible. Impassioned displays of human emotions and crowded rooms are counterproductive for animals who are passing away, and they need to be surrounded with vibrations of loving strength and serenity). I was deeply grateful that Reiki was allowed to be an important part of Franky's passing.

On the morning of December 8, 2011, I laid out a beautiful crystal grid for Franky in my treatment room. At the top was a wheel of blue angelite to facilitate contact with Angels. Surrounding his picture were rose quartz stones engraved with the sacred Usui Reiki symbols, the love energy of the rose quartz amplified with clear quartz points. At the bottom were arrows of black kyanite for protection, balance, and clearing of negativity, flanked by more rose quartz.

Many Angels and Archangels were called in to assist Franky together with Jesus, Mother Mary, and other spiritual beings. I used crystals of lepidolite, a stone which helps transition the soul from incarnation to Light, and selenite, a stone of protection, purification, and Divine light. I felt a discordant dark energy between Franky's shoulder blades which was the energetic signature of his cancer. I was able to remove a portion of this to provide him some relief. Franky had no questions when I explained that today he would be taking his journey. He understood and was prepared.

At the hospital, Franky was calm and accepting. He had already begun to detach from his body and started the transition process on his own. He was ready to go. He patiently accepted some final Crystal Reiki. I asked if he had anything he wanted me to tell the people at the shelter, and he replied, "That I love them." He was very glad that his life had brought him to the shelter which he considered his haven and his home. He informed me that he would begin a mission in spirit of finding other dogs who needed the shelter and bringing them to Martha, the shelter director.

The spirit of Buster entered the room and stood waiting to the left of the door. (Buster is discussed in an earlier case study). Franky looked at him repeatedly, understanding that Buster was meeting him for the journey. Within several seconds of receiving the injection of pentobarbital, Franky's soul leapt up out of his body and appeared as a strong and youthful white dog who shook himself vigorously before joining Buster. I kept my hands on Franky's body, sending out Reiki energy to continue strengthening and helping his soul.

After several minutes, I became aware of a very large energetic presence. I believe this was the primordial spirit called The Guardian of Souls who safeguards the souls of animals on their transitional journeys from life to Light. I then saw a very long and winding tunnel of a smoky orange substance through which Franky's soul was traveling rapidly, a light shining ahead in the distance. He came out from the tunnel into a vista of brilliant golden light, and I knew that he had arrived safely where he was meant to go.

I was deeply thankful Franky permitted me to witness his sacred voyage. Following is a picture of Franky's crystal grid. After he crossed over, I lit an Angel candle to honor his gentle soul.

My work with Franky is the essence of everything this book sets forth. A soul being of sentient intelligence and sensitivity, Franky made an impact during his lifetime which reached beyond his own little corner of the world. His soul *is* present in the Afterlife, making an even greater impact from the Spiritual Realm. I know, because I have seen him there.

On the night of December 11, 2011, a time of an eclipse of the full moon, I gathered with a group of shamans and healers for a special evening of shamanic journeying. Franky's soul joined me ahead of the first journey, walking right into the room and getting into my lap as soon as the leading shaman had "rattled in the spirits." The room was filled with the sound of chanting, singing, and dancing not created by the lone drummer and his human companions.

Franky and I journeyed up to meet a Native American war party in the High Desert, chanting and dancing in a spiraling line around their fire, the warrior braves stretching up onto a shelf of rock above us as the moon shone down. I was told to mount a horse and join this war party, and I resisted, wanting this night to be about peace and entering into the higher vibration of 2012. The spirits were adamant, however, and with Franky in my arms, I mounted a horse and joined the war party on their ride through the nighttime desert.

It was then that I saw our true mission – we were Warriors of Light, the Light Bringers, and I joined the others in war cries as we threw etheric spears of light that illuminated the darkness around us, bringing forth clarity of detail and a dispelling of the veil. Franky and I – animal and human – the Indians and horses – animals and humans – were *together* these Light Bringers.

(Interestingly, my husband Ben, another journeyer at the gathering, traveled at the same time with his canine Spirit Guide to the realm Ben calls "Doggie Heaven." He asked if Franky was there and was told that no, Franky was not currently in that realm because he was too busy with many things to do that night)!

When humans and animals act as a conjoined force, we step fully into our power as Children of the Divine. Animals are here to remind human beings who we are, and once we remember and take up our higher purpose, they will be our faithful partners, companions, supporters, teachers, and healers along the Way.

The Animal Lightworkers

In a fascinating session with my dear friend and collaborator, psychic medium Suzette Schmidt, she channeled information from "The Marys" (Mother Mary and Mary Magdalene) about a group of animals coming into being today called The Animal Lightworkers. It has been revealed that more and more animals are coming through, incarnating at this time in history to assist with the work of the transformational energies bombarding the Earth and opening a way for human and animal evolution. These animals have more of a purpose than just being our companions; indeed, they are on a Divine spiritual mission.

The Animal Lightworkers are coming here to help us identify the connections between creatures rather than focusing on the divisions. Hand in paw, they are coming to lead us back to the loving Universal God whom they have always known.

What is our role in this? For me, it includes connecting with people who have a more Enlightened point of view about the Animal Kingdom. Some of these people will want their animals to be of greater service to the world and will want to learn how to identify and further the personal Divine missions of their animals. Others will want to learn lessons of spiritual power from their animal companions and let their animals help them get onto their spiritual path or get in touch with their true life purpose. Still others will be seeking healing both for themselves and their animal families.

Suzette has learned that both she and I will be connecting humans and Animal Lightworkers with each other and to their service work as well as collaborating with them. If you feel a personal calling towards animal spirituality and how humans and animals can become more integrated in their spiritual work, this is a path you should explore. Your first step begins with the animals in your own life who are waiting for that partnership.

Spiritual Services and Prayers for Animals

This section includes samples of spiritual and religious services and observances which can be performed for animals as well as meditative prayers for blessing and assistance.

- The first is a memorial service which I prepared for a friend's dog. I included information from our final distance crystal Reiki session as well as poetry, words of memorial, and channeled messages which were read at his memorial service.

- The second is a sample crystal grid used to honor and commune with a transitioned animal soul at the Eve of All Hallows, a time traditionally thought of in regard to human souls.

- Third is a service of blessing to welcome a new animal family member. This could easily be adapted to celebrate the birth of a new litter.

- Lastly is a selection of prayers for animals in need.

In Memory of
Buddy Schmidt – Beloved Dog

Buddy's Crystal Reiki Grid
April 15, 2012

This grid includes: Lepidolite (eases soul transition), angelite and celestite (invokes Angelic presences), clear quartz (energy amplifier, master healer), rose quartz (heart chakra, love energies, Divine Feminine), and selenite (auric cleanser, amplifies the grid, resonates with White Light energies).

Buddy was prepared to calmly make his transition at the time of this session. His Life Force energy was low; I sensed that the transitional process had been set in motion. I did rose quartz crystal wand massage and sent Reiki for the greatest healing and comfort possible in the situation at all levels of body, mind, and spirit. Through the wanding process, I received impressions of blood in the stool and a clear anatomic picture of his lungs. There was no indication of pain or suffering. Buddy was not afraid. I offered him reassurance and assistance.

I asked if there were any messages for Suzette, and he wanted to say that she was at the center of his world, showing a figure around which was drawn an orange circle of light. I saw images of peacock feathers. I also saw my Spirit Guide hold a bird to her lips and release it into flight; I understood this to be a metaphor for Buddy's soul. I asked for Divine care and keeping of Buddy's soul at this time, and Mother Mary appeared to cradle Buddy's soul in her arms. I knew that he had the highest level of Divine support and protection.

I did not understand the imagery of the peacock feathers but Animal Speak *by Ted Andrews states the keynote of this bird is* "resurrection and wise vision," *the pattern of eyes in the feathers representing watchfulness, wisdom, and a greater vision. He goes on to state that,* "Of all birds, the peacock most resembles the traditional descriptions of the phoenix...the legendary bird that is sacrificed in the fires of life and then rises from the flames out of its own ashes." (p. 182, Andrews, 1993)

Significant for Buddy, a dog who often licked and bit at his calloused paws (what he called his "grumpy toes"), Andrews remarks that this bird is known for its ugly feet, said to screech each time he catches site of them. "For anyone with a peacock as a totem, an examination of the mysticism and symbolism of feet should be examined." (p. 182, Andrews, 1993)

Shortly after Buddy's soul left his body, I sat under the bare sky in the sun and wind to send him Reiki for his soul transition. I saw golden fronds of light like an aurora borealis, sometimes coalescing into forms like branches laden with golden blossoms or golden fields of wheat blowing in a breeze. I then saw an image that resembled the solar disk with

rays of light streaming out around it, and I realized that this was a portal of light. Standing to the left was a black and white Great Dane who turned and looked at me; I had the impression of a canine Guardian Spirit or Gatekeeper. I then saw Buddy walk up alongside him, and they entered into the light together, all the streaming rays returning into the central core of the portal as the Great Gate closed behind them. Buddy had arrived safely to the Golden Realm of the Spirit.

A Dog's Journey

A golden boy, he crossed through the Golden Door
found beyond the panoply of light-worked sky,
feet as sure upon the ethers as the floor
beneath the Tibetan rug on which he'd lie.

For Buddy spoke the many tongues of creatures
who are wise in ways of heart and mind and soul,
and carefully he'd memorized the features
of the ones he'd come to comfort and console.

Playful, bold, inquisitive spirit of joy,
a romp in the grass or a chase of the ball
were a balm to the heart of sweet Buddy boy,
as eager to roam as come back at a call.

Companion, friend, confidante in comfort wise,
he taught of wonder and of love without an end.
His sweet soul was ever shining from his eyes,

in the sacred body nature thought to lend.

Now a Spirit Guide who crossed the path of light,
he bounds unfettered, so swift and sure and fleet
as he swoops and soars with angels in their flight
in the Realm of Spirit where the air is sweet.

For it is the way of life, and death, and birth
that the body passes, but the Jewel it holds
rises up into the Life beyond the Earth
where the endless peace of Oneness then unfolds.

The golden boy beyond his golden portal,
distant as the stars, close as every heartbeat –
this is the way when life becomes immortal
and death but another door though which we meet.

Buddy, blessed be until we meet again.

Channeled Messages from Buddy Schmidt
Received April 19, 2012

Channeled by Elizabeth S. Eiler, Ph.D.

- *Suzette, I am a protector for you. Whenever you see the sheltering arms of trees, think of me.*

- *To my family: I love you, and I want you to be happy.*

- *Suzette, I want to help you be successful.*

- *Be peaceful with the Angels of the Earth.*

- *Buddy thanked me for helping him and appeared in the company of Angels. He showed me images of a place filled with rainbow-colored arches of light and beautiful trumpeting swans. He said that he is happy and is free.*

- *Buddy shared happy memories of lying in the living room, enjoying the energy of the crystals in the house. He barked and looked at me intently wanting me to convey his desire for you to communicate with him and know that he is still here.*

Words of Memorial – April 20, 2012

We ask for blessing of the beloved soul of Buddy in the name of the Father, the Son, and the Holy Spirit.

We also ask for the divine blessing of the Mother, for it was Mother Mary who reached out her arms to accept and embrace Buddy's sweet soul.

We give special thanks to Buddy's Angelic guardians and helpers and to the animal Spirit Guides who assisted him throughout his life and during the process of his transition.

We give thanks for Buddy's life and for the golden opportunity to exchange love and companionship with this special dog. We learned much from his unique blend of wisdom, humor, and character, and the world is a better place for Buddy's life and the love that always surrounded him and radiated from him.

That the Earth's variety of creatures can share such a bond of precious love with one another is yet one more proof of the Divine truth of Unity of all life and Godspark in all creation. Blessed be the sweet soul of Buddy until we know the joy of our reunion with his eternal essence. We ask this in the Name of the Most Holy God. Amen.

Eve of All Hallows: Moving Closer to their Souls

Halloween is a wonderful time to reconnect with the souls of beloved animals who have made the life-to-Light transition to the realm of Spirit and are closer to us than ever at this changeling season. This is a time for animals far removed from the hissing black cats or vampire bats of pop culture. It is a powerful spiritual time in our earthly calendar whose mysteries can be shared equally among the birds of the air, the beasts of the field, the fishes in the deeps, and human beings.

The Eve of All Hallows marks a mystical point at the turning of the seasons when the veils between the worlds grow thin, and we move closer to the realms of Other. The old Celtic traditions held that "in-between places" (riverbanks, forest glades) and "in-between times" (dusk, dawn, seasonal shifts) made for easier access through the dimensional portals to places outside of ordinary time and space. In Christianity, November 1st and 2nd are All Saints' Day and All Souls' Day, and Christians around the globe visit graves, light candles, leave flowers, and commemorate the spirits of the dead.

The dance from spring into summer, fall, winter, and the coming of spring again is particularly poignant and meaningful in that it mirrors the endless life-to-death-to-life cycle of all created beings undergoing physical incarnations. As we move from mid-summer into fall, when all Nature's bounty goes down to sleep in one last blaze of glory, we move inexorably towards the limbo time of winter, when the Beloved has passed away into the wind, and long months of darkness and cold prepare the way for blessed rebirth.

Animals sense these changes in the air – and even in the dimensional fabric – in all their subtleties and variations, and they pay homage, going still amidst all the preparations of digging dens and storing food and laying on fat. I see it in my dog's eyes when he stops and takes the air, listening and feeling for all the shades of difference. This time of All Souls is for our animal companions, too.

Above is a photo of a simple layout for meditation to assist with contacting the soul of a deceased animal loved one. A photograph is the focus, but you might wish to use an urn of cremation ashes or a piece of cremation jewelry. Above the dog's head is rose quartz which opens the heart chakra and strengthens the vibration of love. On the remaining three sides of the picture are amethyst crystals to enhance psychic vision and stimulate spiritual awareness. An angel sits at the top of the layout flanked by white candles to honor the purity of spirit and as an invocation of Divine Light dispelling darkness.

You may enhance the layout in any way you wish – for example, placing the items on the dog or cat's blanket, adding a favorite toy or collar, placing religious or spiritual symbols, or adding beautiful autumn elements like red maple leaves or a branch of berries. Some other stones to use include angelite or celestite for contacting the Angelic Realm, lapis lazuli or blue kyanite for communication, and pink tourmaline or rhodonite for love energy. You might want to create a layout for several animals. What is most important is your intention to honor and connect with each animal in spirit, going into a place of deep meditation and higher awareness where the fog of distractions is dispelled and precious contacts made.

Meditate on the enduring qualities of love on Halloween, and spend some time reconnecting with a much-missed departed soul. Herein lies the true purpose and usefulness of this turn of the seasons, and an opportunity to restore meaning to a worn out and misunderstood cultural icon.

Blessing As The Family Grows
An instant to conceive, a lifetime to cherish,
an eternity to love.

Beloved spirit, beautiful child of God, we celebrate your life here with us and welcome you fully into our family circle.

- We promise to answer your loyalty with loyalty and your love with love.

- We promise nurture:
  - Food and water
  - Vaccines and prevention
  - Love and companionship
  - Training and play
  - Medical care for your health and comfort.

- We pledge to keep you safe.

- We promise to teach you all you need to know for success.

- We will help you belong.

- We will be patient and forgiving as you will be with our mistakes.

- We promise to be firm but gentle.

- We will be quick to celebrate your goodness and your milestones.

- We will love you forever.

♥ This is your forever home.

- We ask our Good and Loving God to bless and protect this one, (animal's name) and (his/her) family as they embark on life's journey together.

- We ask that You gather Your loving, guiding Angels around this family, and we especially ask for Guardian Angels to be assigned to (animal's name) for (his/her) lifetime for special loving care and protection.

- Blessed Be this family circle – (names of all human and animal family members are spoken) – and may they know the full Unity of Joy which transcends all time and space and is eternal.

WE ASK AND PROMISE ALL THESE THINGS IN THE NAME OF OUR DIVINE SOURCE AND LOVING GOD. AMEN.

Prayer for Healing

Divine and Healing God, I ask you to please place Your hands upon (your animal's name) to impart the highest level of healing possible in this situation. I ask for healing at the physical, emotional, mental, and soul levels. I even ask boldly for a miracle if such is for the highest good of all concerned.

I ask God and the Angels to assist the veterinarians to reach the correct diagnosis and implement the best treatment plan. Please empower any medications and procedures to be of the greatest help possible to (your animal's name).

Archangel Michael, please banish whatever is harmful to my animal. With your powerful sword, please extract any darkness or negativity from my animal's physical and energetic bodies, replacing these structures with your beams of amethyst light to purify and protect.

Archangel Raphael, I ask you to fill my animal loved one's body with your powerful emerald light, casting out all illness and infirmity. Rcplacc sickncss with hcalth and rcplacc sluggishness with vitality at every level of (your animal's name)'s being. Bolster (his/her) energies for the highest and most powerful healing with your therapeutic emerald illumination.

I pray for relief of any pain or suffering and for total peace and comfort of body, mind, emotions, and spirit. I ask that all be done for the greatest good and most merciful benefit of (your animal's name).

Amen.

Prayer Before a Medical Procedure

Dear God who is our Great Physician, please guide the veterinary team who will work with my animal companion today.

Let it be Your hands that direct the doctor's hands and Your compassion that fills the hearts of all who will care for (your animal's name).

I ask You to empower (your animal's name)'s Guardian Angels to watch over (him/her) with especial care today.

I also call upon the protecting presence of Archangel Michael and the healing presence of Archangel Raphael to shed their light on my beloved animal companion at this time.

I pray for the highest and best outcome for (your animal's name) from this procedure, and I ask for (him/her) to know comfort and peace throughout.

Amen.

Prayer for a Lost Animal

Archangel Raphael, special protector and guide for lost animals, I ask you to assist in reuniting (your animal's name) with (his/her) loving family as soon as possible. Whether (your animal's name) is guided to return home or we are led to find (him/her), I ask for your help in bringing us quickly and safely together once more.

I ask you to protect (him/her) from any harm or danger and to put kind and helpful people in (his/her) path. Please ensure that (your animal's name) is met only with compassion and caring and is quickly brought to safety. I ask you to see that all of (his/her) basic needs are met while we are apart.

I pray for (your animal's name)'s safe and speedy homecoming and request that you and your Angelic team provide the highest level of empowerment for this process. Please illuminate the path that will bring us together again and keep our feet firmly upon it.

Amen.

Prayer for Guidance

Dear God, please assist me in gaining higher insight into the needs of (your animal's name) at this time. Grant me the wisdom of understanding and the compassion to make the right decisions.

Archangel Gabriel, help me to communicate with my animal companion in a way of love and integrity. Empower the expression of (his/her) truth and open my eyes, ears, and heart that I may see, hear, and know what (your animal's name) has to convey.

St. Francis, help me to know our little brothers and sisters as you did, and guide me in the most loving course of action. Please assist me in carrying out the highest and best process for (your animal's name).

I ask that all barriers or difficulties to the most beneficial solution be removed at this time.

I ask for God and the Angels to bring to me the people who can be of the most benefit by their knowledge, expertise, and skills. I desire these helpful souls to enter my life as soon as possible.

Dear God, by Divine help, please keep us all on the path of truth and loving resolution.

Amen.

Prayer at the End of Life

Dear God, Divine Author of life and Keeper of every soul,
I ask for You to gently shepherd my beloved (your animal's name) on (his/her) final journey off the Earth plane.
Surround (him/her) with the highest-level Divine beings
for love, protection, guidance, and support during the soul
transition process.

Give aid and strength to (your animal's name)'s Guardian
Angels as they perform their final mission for this sweet
soul, and surround (him/her) with a loving host of Angelic
guides and protectors.

Dear God, I ask You to banish forever any dark or negative
presences that would approach (your animal's name), and I
ask for Archangel Michael and his Angelic army to prevent
any interference with (his/her) smooth and safe transition
from life to Light and the higher Realms thereafter.

Dear God, Mother Mary, St. Francis, and Archangel Ariel,
suffuse my beloved (your animal's name) with deep peace,
confidence, love, and joy. Please hold (him/her) in your arms
of Light and provide all that is needed at every level.

Strengthen my faith in the true knowledge that our souls
are eternal and the essence of humans and animals is im-
perishable. Comfort me and (your animal's name) with the
assurance that our love will continue everlastingly and that
our soul reunion in the Realm of Spirit is assured.

Amen.

How You Can Help Animals

Begin with the animals in your own home. Healing the relationship between humans and animals starts at the most personal level. Remember always to cherish the animals in your care. Learn to communicate with them. Devote time to training, play, and simple companionship. Feed a high-quality diet, obtain proper veterinary care (including vaccinations, flea and tick prevention, heartworm prevention, etc.), and keep your animals clean and well-groomed. Provide a clean, safe home and a secure play yard. Please do not allow your animals to procreate unless you can personally guarantee a responsible home for every animal born as a result. My personal preference is to spay/neuter due to the extreme overpopulation of animals leading to homelessness, suffering, and death.

Do not ever buy animals from pet stores, backyard breeders, or newspaper and Internet ads. "Pet store puppies" are often supplied by puppy mills, places of torture and suffering for animals. Remember, purchasing a puppy mill dog puts money into the hands of the dog's abusers. The way to rescue puppy mill dogs is to pass laws prohibiting inhumane breeding and housing of animals – and then to enforce the law with investigations and raids carried out by police in partnership with legitimate animal rescue groups. You can adopt dogs rescued from puppy mills by contacting The Humane Society of the United States, the ASPCA, Petfinder.com, and licensed animal shelters.

Shelter animals are not homeless because they are bad; most of them are homeless because their people let them down. I always recommend shelter adoption as a first choice for finding an animal companion. Traditional shelters place every animal on death row the moment she arrives. Not adopted in time, countless innocent cats, dogs, rabbits, and other animals in local shelters are euthanized to make room for the constant influx of homeless and abandoned "pets." You literally save a life every time you adopt from a shelter.

- **SUPPORT HOMELESS ANIMALS:** Please support Animal Lifeline of Iowa, a special-needs, no-kill shelter accepting animals with medical problems, illnesses, serious injuries, and in need of immediate care. The shelter rescues animals suffering from abuse and abandonment, and provides a safe haven for pregnant or nursing moms and babies and orphans requiring bottle-feeding. These animals would not survive without Animal Lifeline. Please visit their website today at http: //www.animal-lifeline.com/index.html.

- **STOP PUPPY MILLS:** To learn more about puppy mills and how you can help shut down these cruel places and rescue animal victims, please visit The Humane Society of the United States at http://www.humanesociety.org/issues/puppy_mills.

- **ANIMAL CARE:** For tips on how to care for dogs, cats, horses, and small animals (including advice on nutrition, training, poison control, and more), please visit the ASPCA at http://www.aspca.org/Home/Pet-care.aspx.

Bibliography

Andrews, Ted (1993). *Animal Speak: The Spiritual & Magical Powers of Creatures Great & Small.* Woodbury, MN: Llewellyn Publications.

Coates, Margrit (2003). *Hands-on Healing for Pets: The Animal Lover's Essential Guide to Using Healing Energy.* London, England: Rider Books.

Craft, Karen (2011). Animal communication workshop led by Karen Craft and attended by Elizabeth Eiler, May 1, 2011.

Fulton, Elizabeth and Prasad, Kathleen (2006). *Animal Reiki: Using energy to heal the animals in your life.* Berkeley, CA: Ulysses Press.

Guerrero, Diana L. (2003). *What Animals Can Teach Us about Spirituality.* Woodstock, VT: SkyLight Paths Publishing.

Jacobs, Alan (2011). Interview by Elizabeth Eiler with Alan Jacobs, July 5, 2011.

Scott, Martin J. and Mariani, Gael (2002). *Crystal Healing for Animals.* Scotland, UK: Findhorn Press.

Stein, Diane (1995). *Essential Reiki: A Complete Guide to an Ancient Healing Art.* Berkeley, CA: Crossing Press.

What Is Reiki? (n.d.). The International Center for Reiki Training. Retrieved July 4, 2011 from http://www.reiki. org/FAQ/WhatIsReiki.html

Woolcott, Ina (n.d.). *Alligator/Crocodile Power Animal, Symbol of Primal Energies, Survival.* Retrieved May 5, 2012 from http://www.shamanicjourney.com/article/6197/alligator-crocodile-power-animal-symbol-of-primal-energies-survival.

CPSIA information can be obtained at www.ICGtesting.com
Printed in the USA
LVOW131838041012

301529LV00015B/96/P